AIDA
OF LENINGRAD

AIDA
OF LENINGRAD

THE STORY OF AIDA SKRIPNIKOVA

Edited by
Xenia Howard-Johnston and Michael Bourdeaux

GATEWAY OUTREACH

ACKNOWLEDGEMENTS

THE EDITORS wish to thank Miss Kathleen Matchett and David Knight for their help in translating the trial of Aida Skripnikova.

Thanks are also due to the *Sunday Telegraph* for their kind permission to reproduce the material contained in the 'Epilogue'.

First published in 1972 *by*
GATEWAY OUTREACH
60 *London St., Reading, Berkshire, England*

Printed in Great Britain at
THE ABBEY PRESS
Abingdon, Berkshire

ISBN 0 901644 09 9

CONTENTS

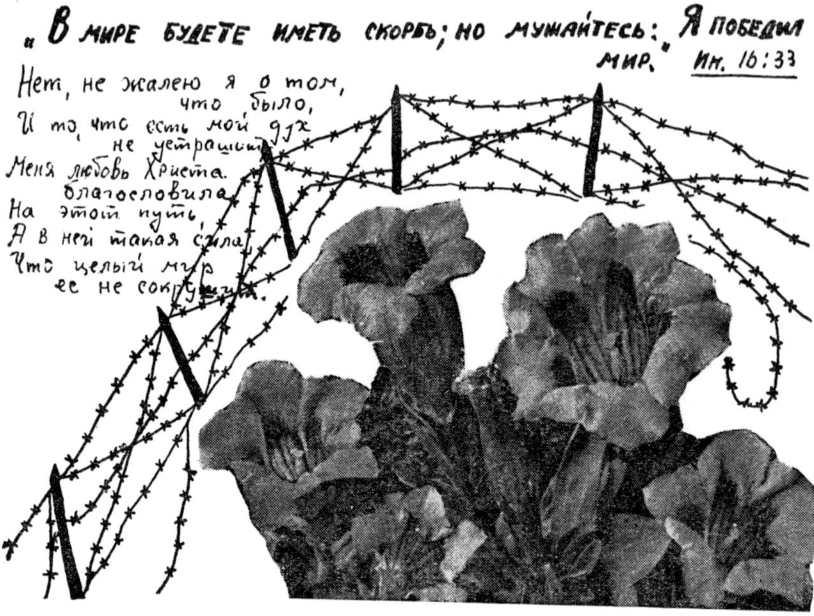

A card sent from prison by Aida.

The wording on the front reads as follows:—

"In the world you will have tribulation; but be of good courage: I have overcome the world." *John* 16:33

> No, I do not hanker after the past,
> And the present does not frighten my spirit.
> The love of Christ blessed me on my way,
> And the power in this love is such
> That not even the whole world can destoy it.

Summary of the story, written by Aida on the inside pages

Nadezhda [hope] is in prison: it is Christmas, and as she looks out of the small opening at the sky from her cell, she sings praises to God for the birth of the Christ. A worn, dispirited middle-aged woman asks Nadezhda why the world is so full of injustice. To this Nadezhda replies with the parable of the Prodigal Son, explaining that it is man who has chosen to abandon God and bring unhappiness upon himself. If man would return to God, he would discover joy. The older woman asks Nadezhda if she knows this joy even in prison, and she answers "Yes".

FOREWORD

by Brother Andrew

God forbid that this book should be another piece of Christian entertainment.

It should be highly disturbing because every aspect of Aida's suffering was caused by our own failure . . . not simply by failure to understand but by a vast array of failures on the part of Christians which have literally caused this world to split into two parts.

Many Christians have died for their faith in Jesus in this generation.

What is wrong?

The main problem is that we did not prevent this from happening, and now that it has happened we are not identifying ourselves with those who are being abused for Jesus' sake.

Consequently the world is going to hell.

But God . . .
takes an Aida to show the whole Church how to reverse this deadly trend.

And Paul . . .
writing to the Romans (ch. 1:5) says that his ministry is "to bring about the obedience of faith for the sake of His name among all the nations."
We have faith.
Aida has "the obedience of faith". And that made her a criminal.
What was her crime?
She stood on the street corners of the Nevsky Prospekt in Leningrad and gave out hand-written Gospel tracts. There were no nicely printed tracts available because we did not supply the Russian believers with the tools to break the power of atheism.
Aida did it all by herself. She knew that because she tried to fight the battle against atheism single-handed she would be

severely punished. She also knew that this, and nothing else, would bring personal freedom to her and to her beloved country ultimately.

The battle was spiritual and that is the way she fought it. Our failure is that we did not identify ourselves with her and with those whom she represents. We did not protest and I dare say that very few believers even missed a single meal to pray for or financially support the work done in that country to relieve the suffering.

Yet there is no other way. Unless we identify ourselves with those who are blazing the trail, like Aida and many of Russia's suffering Christians there will simply be no Kingdom of God no matter how advanced our theology may be regarding this subject.

Then: Rise up and stand in the gap. "Recall the former days when, after you were enlightened, you endured a hard struggle with suffering, sometimes being publicly exposed to abuse and affliction, sometimes being *partners* with those so treated." So says God's Word in Hebrews 10:32 and 33.

Aida is paying the price for Russia and the whole world.

Are we praying?

Am I?

Ermelo, Holland,
October 1972

I

A PERSONAL MEMOIR

by S. L. Robertson

I met Aida in August 1961 and again between September 1963 and June 1964. All I write here is at her behest. Aida's prime concern was that Christians in the West should be made aware of the true position of Soviet believers.

"Still waters run deep," goes the English proverb; the Russian one says, "Still waters undermine the riverbanks". This is the kind of phrase used by Soviet literature and atheist propaganda when referring to believers of the reformed faith. Official policy towards religion has oscillated between persecution and a minimum tolerance of its existence. "Peaceful coexistence" applied to Soviet foreign policy has no place at home, especially concerning belief in God. It is important to remember this at a time when many are tempted to go along with Communist ideology as "fellow-travellers" attracted by the social and economic goals of the USSR which have much that springs from humanitarian concern.

In the Soviet Union today (where, since 1968 a Civil Rights movement has grown up) many are demanding recognition of individual rights. It is against the background of this movement that we must see the demand by believers for religious freedom. When believers ask that they be allowed to meet for prayer and fellowship in private homes, the Soviet authorities claim that anti-Soviet activities are being fomented at these meetings, and insist that believers meet only in the registered churches or "prayer houses" provided by the State.

The spiritual element in human life, which ought to be central, has been redefined in social and political terms: "Man is the measure of all things" sums up well what the Soviet state expects of its citizens, whether believers or not. The goal of (material) progress leaves no room for those seeking the inner life. Religion is condemned as promoting passivity and subservience. The Kazan Cathedral in Leningrad, now a museum, has its walls amply decorated with texts from the Bible, designed to show how Christians are encouraged to abdicate from their responsibilities in the physical realm. You read quotations like: "Slaves, submit to your masters", or see illustrations equating toil with God's curse on mankind.

In August 1961 I visited, on three occasions, the Baptist church in Leningrad. Once, after the service, a girl approached me. She seemed anxious to learn and was seeking an explanation to the doubts within her. I told her to speak to the pastor, who would surely be able to help her through regular contact.

The girl, Aida Skripnikova, said that the pastor had no time for such a thing. This struck me then as a little odd. After the service we walked back to town and I tried to explain to her what was meant by being a Christian. I gave her two or three gospels which I had brought with me. Limited as the ministry was that I could offer, she hung on to every word. I felt as though I was someone trying to light a match in the middle of a dark forest.

Main towns in the USSR generally have just one legal meeting-place, but even here the believers are sometimes subject to harassment. The Leningrad church, which is situated at the edge of the city in an old Orthodox church – used later as a workshop – has, on a Sunday morning, the constant accompaniment of motor cycles revving round and round the building. It was here that I came in September 1963, after a lengthy tram-ride across town. Having stood in the tramcar for an hour I might have relished the thought of a seat – but there are no seats in a Russian church!

After the service, which lasted over two hours, Aida came rushing up to me and told me that she was now a Christian. Her brother was a believer (he had since died) and she was tremendously impressed with his life and at last came to the point of faith. Also since we had last met, she had been hauled up before a Comrades' Court[1] and questioned on her contact with a certain foreigner after church on Sundays. She was warned that if she went on in her Christian ways, she would be brought to trial and sentenced. For this, Aida said, she was fully prepared, but witness she must.

1. An informal—though legal—way of administering justice for lesser offences, where a person is tried by workers of his own area.

I truly enjoyed worshipping with Russian Christians: the Spirit of Christ was present. The Word was preached, albeit always in the same basic terms. It was a real change from daily Soviet life, where to name the name of Christ brought at least mirth, if not total unbelief. Nevertheless there were many among Soviet youth who asked more searching questions and came secretly to church – secretly, that is, from their friends and fellow-students.

It became apparent that all was not as it seemed superficially: Aida went around with lists of names of imprisoned Christians. She spoke of "trusting the pastor *more than* the elders" – talk which I found strange. The pastor in his prayers thanked God for a congress held to cleanse the church at which important resolutions were passed. Aida seemed so much more involved in all this than other Christians. Above all, she was fearless in approaching others, particularly foreigners, and asking for their help. Her constant theme was that of appealing to Western Christians for help. It may be that, with the knowledge we have of the situation, we shall have much to answer for before the Throne of Grace for lack of prayer on behalf of our brethren.

Aida was secretary of a group known as the Organizing Committee[2] or *Orgkomitet.* The aim of this committee was to prepare for a congress of the church to cleanse it of impure elements and make it concentrate entirely on its spiritual functions.

Local Christians in Leningrad used to urge Aida to go on with her studies, as indeed did we foreigners, but her sight was set on higher things and she wanted only to further the cause of Christ and His people in the USSR. She regarded Leningrad believers as too timorous and left her job to go to the Ukraine to gather material "for external use". She came back in the spring of 1964, saying how bold were the believers in the south.

She stayed with her sister while away from Leningrad and learned that the police were trying to catch her as she left the

2. This committee was at first (1961) called the Action Group. (*Initsiativnaya gruppa,* shortened to *Initsiativniki,* the name by which these reformers are most commonly known. 'Reform Baptists' is the best English equivalent).

Ukraine for Leningrad. She saw them stationed at the bus and rail terminals, so she took a country bus in the opposite direction and reached Leningrad by a devious route. Having given up her job there earlier, she automatically lost her right to have a residence permit for Leningrad and had to be sheltered outside the city. Wisely or unwisely she sometimes came to the students' hostel where I was living and this fact was duly noted. I think it must be said that what she did, she did because she could do no other.

One problem she encountered was the language barrier. She frequently approached foreigners, as already mentioned, to request them to take out material. Naturally this was hard for a visitor to the church to understand, and many of them spoke no Russian. Aida tells how much greater was their astonishment when the elders tried to restrain her physically from approaching the foreigners. They tried to take the papers in her handbag which contained, for example, a list of imprisoned believers.

How could the official organs deal with this kind of situation? The main way was to invite visitors before and after the service to the vestry where questions could be put to the pastor who assured them that anything he said could be recorded. I myself had wondered at this excessive politeness in insisting that I come and sit with the elders, when the only other seats were a few benches occupied by those who reached church very early. Naturally I did not always avail myself of the invitation.

I myself was upset at this conduct of the pastors, and so came to understand why Aida behaved as she did. Later I came to see that our only weapons are prayer and fasting, and that His love alone can conquer in such a situation. This must have been how Aida felt, though to a greater extent, about the church and country she loved.

She and some others are struggling against pitiful odds, having so little, but having Him. We in the West must be involved at depth with the Church Universal. When was the eye ever able to say to the ear "I have no need of you"?

"Scientific atheism" is the name given to anti-religious propaganda. It claims that science and religion are opposed, that the latter foments backward and depraved attitudes. Believers may or may not hold an evolutionary (in the Darwinian sense) view of man, but they believe in man as created by and for God. It is natural then that Russian Christians are as law-abiding and hard-working as other citizens, regardless of the theological definition of the word "toil".

Not infrequently the Christian in a work team turns out the best product or overfulfils his norm to a greater extent than others. How is he to be treated, when it comes to prizes and bonuses? One Christian was in this position. An argument such as the following arose:

– He is a believer; we can't give him the prize!

– He's done the best work, hasn't he?

In the end he received the award.

In the above there is room for agreement or disagreement as the case may be. There is no quarter, however, for underground pastors or full-time Christian workers like Aida who give up secular employment. They are regarded as "parasites", after the proverb "He who does not work shall not eat". When Aida returned from the Ukraine and had to live outside Leningrad, the only work she could get was bottling milk twelve hours a day for about thirty roubles (£13) a month – the very lowest of wages. This she accepted without grumbling.

What strikes one above all else about Aida is her intense love and zeal for her Lord and country. It is the selfless outpouring of her being that is her strength; only such dedication can match the onslaught of people imbued with the ideals of Marxism-Leninism. There is one very good reason for this. If a social goal for Christianity is preached, then it has nothing to offer in the face of communism. Even the pursuit of Christian ideals and ethics is insufficient; each and every Christian must be filled with the power of Jesus Christ and be directed by Him. It seems to me that Aida did not see this in many visitors from abroad.

We used not, at first, to understand each other, I think for the above reasons. Aida could not comprehend how others were not caught up as she was. The restraining voice of other Christians was not for her. Seeing the fields "white unto harvest", she was unable simply to stand and watch.

To a Westerner she might seem outspoken, challenging what one does or does not do. I think she found it difficult to accept that we, enjoying freedom to worship, did so little for those who depend so much on our prayers and help of other kinds. We did not fully understand the importance she attached to informing Western Christians about the situation of believers. She thought our newspapers would devote whole editions to publishing facts about the persecuted church. From her point of view, why should we not? If someone attacks us in the press, we can expect the right to reply. Aida, as a Soviet believer, does not have this possibility.

Our Soviet brothers and sisters ask for our support in prayer and in giving, particularly Bibles; we need their support equally and one way of letting them speak is to publish their message to us.

The Soviet Union has a number of slogans relating to the building of Communism. One of these is familiar to Christian ears: "From each according to his capabilities – to each according to his need". This we see practised by the early Christians. Christ said, "Man shall not live by bread alone, but by every word proceeding from God". His temptation was to lay aside the spiritual task for which He had come, and make "rice Christians". This same temptation, or weapon, is used to entice Christians in Russia away from their spiritual allegiance to Christ. There are those in extreme circumstances who deny their Lord – again a test we have not had to face. I think too that we also miss out on the joy written all over the faces of Aida and other believers: a spiritual joy granted by the Lord to those who have suffered for Him. Whatever else is added to them, they seek first His Kingdom.

Aida did receive that prison sentence and, I am quite sure, was not silent even when thus physically restricted. Will we remember her, who has borne her share of Christ's sufferings and who shall yet share His glory?

York, March 1972.

II

THE BACKGROUND

by MICHAEL BOURDEAUX

THE COMMUNIST movement today is no longer united, everywhere adhering to the same ideological tenets. There have been many splits and ideological quarrels. In practice the divergences are even greater. The situation for Christians varies dramatically from one communist country to another: life for a Christian in Yugoslavia is very different from that of a Christian in the USSR; it is different again in Czechoslovakia or China.

The brand of communism which has developed in the USSR is deeply Russian: Lenin, whose ideas have been amalgamated with those of Marx to form the Soviet ideology, known as Marxism-Leninism, belonged to a particular Russian tradition of revolutionary élitist thought and interpreted Marx's ideas for a Russian context. Lenin and his tightly-knit, well-organized Bolshevik party, wished to impose a political system which would control every aspect of a man's life – his emotional, physical, creative and spiritual life. Had the Bolshevik – later named the Communist – Party merely aimed at creating an economic system where everything was held in common, where each person was provided with his needs and gave to the community as much as he could, where there was no private property, then a Christian could have no grounds for conflicting with such a system. But when a political system demands the total control of a man, that he should render unto Caesar that which is God's, then a Christian finds himself in conflict with it.

Christians in the Soviet Union today consider it quite possible for them to live within Soviet society so long as certain rights, guaranteed by the constitution, are observed in practice. The present Article 124 of the Constitution on freedom of conscience originally under Lenin permitted "religious propaganda" as well as anti-religious propaganda. In 1929, however, this phrase was altered to "religious confession" and when a new constitution was drawn up in 1936, it was again changed, this time to "religious worship". Officially this phrase is interpreted to mean that the Christian community may hold services only in a registered building and at a time specified by the state. Were this article to include freedom of religious propaganda, without which, many Christians would argue, there can be no question of true freedom of conscience, then this would grant Christians the freedom they seek. Were the 1918 *Decree of the Council of People's Commissars* respected in practice, Christians in the USSR would be able to live without conflict within Soviet society. This decree lays down that church and state be separate: that the church be allowed to deal with its own internal affairs without interference by the state.

In practice, however, the state in many ways interferes in church affairs in an attempt to control religious life. For example, a Christian community is required to obtain registration from the local *soviet* (council) in its area before it can meet legally. Should a comunity be lucky enough to obtain registration, it is then given a building by the state in which it can hold its services. Unfortunately, it is often the case that a religious community is refused registration, and consequently has nowhere to meet legally. The Orthodox Christians at Naro-Fominsk, near Moscow, have been unsuccessfully applying for registration for over forty years. Such a community is forced to meet in private, in someone's flat, or in the open air, in some forest, but these meetings are considered illegal by the Soviet state and for such action a community can be prosecuted.

The Evangelical Christian and Baptist Churches were founded separately in Russia during the last century. In 1944, after fifteen years of severe persecution, the state established the All-Union Council of the Evangelical Christian and Baptist Church (AUCECB) to unite the two churches under a central organizing body.[1] There were tensions in the Council from the first and some churches never joined at all.

1. Full documentation on this can be found in Michael Bourdeaux, *Religious Ferment in Russia* (Macmillan, London, 1968).

In 1961 a schism ocurred among the Soviet Baptists and its effects are still to be seen.

In 1960 the AUCECB issued the so-called *New Statutes* and the *Letter of Instructions.* They were directed principally to District Superintendents and contained guidance on the practical administration of church life. These new directives, among other things, forbade the attendance of children at divine services, suspended all baptisms of young people under 18 and advised the reduction to a minimum of baptisms of people in the 18-30 age group. "Unhealthy missionary tendencies" were to be restrained.

All these provisions, and indeed the whole tenor of both documents, evoked the opposition of large numbers of Baptists. They called for a congress, to be attended by representatives from all congregations – registered (i.e. legal), unregistered and those from which the Soviet authorities had recently removed registration illegally (e.g. at Brest). In the early 1960's, it was enough for a congregation to challenge the *New Statutes* for its registration and that of its pastor to be removed. Internal church regulations were being used illegally and without any justification as a test of loyalty to the Soviet regime. Sometimes registration of a congregation was removed without even this excuse – and precisely the same happened to thousands of Russian Orthodox, Adventist, Roman Catholic and Jewish congregations at the same time.

The Baptists who opposed this nationwide anti-religious campaign were the "Action Group" (*Initsiativniki*) referred to in Chapter I. We shall call them "reformers". What they were agitating for originally was an all-Union congress which would discuss all these problems which had arisen, and which would call together elected representatives from all registered and unregistered congregations. It was hoped that democratic elections to senior posts would follow for the first time (the state, in fact exercised a veto over these, though there is no provision for this in the law. It does have a legal veto over the people elected by a congregation to represent it at the local level).

Being put under nationwide pressure from Baptists, the state relented, although only to the extent of allowing representatives of registered congregations to meet for a congress in 1963 (and again in 1966 and 1969). The *Letter of Instruc-*

tions was abolished and the *New Statutes* were modified and eventually replaced.[2]

Nevertheless, the mistrust of a leadership which could allow such events as those of 1960 to occur was not alleviated. The reformers continued to call for a fully representative congress with free elections to all posts of authority. This has been resolutely refused by the Soviet authorities, even though such a refusal itself constitutes an illegal intrusion into internal church affairs. In 1965 the reformers formally constituted themselves into a "Council of Churches of the Evangelical Christians and Baptists" and set up their own constitution. The state never recognized this body and has continuously persecuted its leaders, although when two of them, Gennadi Kryuchkov and Georgi Vins, were brought to trial in 1966, the prosecutor admitted that they were *de facto* the elected leaders of a significant Baptist constituency in the USSR.[3]

The persecution of these two men in particular has continued. A letter from Uzlovaya church, near Tula, dated 22 August 1971, speaks of the nationwide search now in progress for Kryuchkov. His photograph hangs on police noticeboards beside those of common criminals. Local officials have intimated to his wife that if he is found and should attempt to escape, he will be shot. There is no doubt that such an "escape attempt" could easily be provoked.

The last few years have seen a widening in the scope of the demands for reform. They began with appeals to the official Baptist leadership. Receiving no satisfactory reply, the reformers turned to the Soviet authorities and were imprisoned for their trouble. Others stepped into their shoes and appealed to the Baptist World Alliance, to the United Nations, the European Parliament in Strasbourg, the International Commission of Jurists, to "all Christians of the world".

The results of the reform movement have also multiplied. Their regular information bulletin, the "Fraternal Leaflet" (*Bratsky Listok*) for July-August 1971, a jubilee issue marking ten years of the movement, spoke of the large financial sacri-

2. A full and popular account of their experience is to be found in the paper-back, *Faith on Trial in Russia* (Hodder and Stoughton, London, 1971).

3. Since then both groups have been commonly referred to as "the Baptists".

fices made by individuals of registered and unregistered congregations, especially for the printing and distribution of literature; of the number of baptisms; of the establishment of an actual printing enterprise called "The Christian", which is said to have produced already over 40,000 copies of the New Testament, hymn books and other religious literature – all this in secret. Such events have never before occurred in the Soviet Union.

At the same time the main venom of the Soviet anti-religious campaign of the 1960's was siphoned off against the reformers, leaving the official body some breathing space, which they exploited and thus – at least to some extent – justified their policy of trying to work within the system. There was a state-approved printing of the Bible and hymn book, an enlarged edition of the only official periodical, "Fraternal Messenger" (*Bratsky Vestnik*), and a new theological correspondence course was established – the first formal religious education for Russian Baptists for forty years.

This first course has now ended with most of its participants achieving the diploma. The official magazine is beginning to report that individuals from it have become pastors or deacons. The next course has now begun.

At the same time, however, intimidation and arrests of the reformers have continued. Sentences in some cases became even harsher than in 1966, when Vins and Kryuchkov were given three years. Thus it was with Trofim Feidak and Vladimir Vilchinsky, resolute leaders of the Brest Baptists, whose registration had been taken away from them in 1960. On 17 April 1968 each was sentenced to five years' imprisonment. Their successor in the leadership of this congregation, Mikhail Bartoshuk, was also arrested on 20 August 1970, and sentenced to five years in a strict-regime labour camp.

A feature of some of the new court cases has been the youth of some of the defendants. Raisa Burmai was arrested in the Ukraine in 1968 when she was a mere seventeen, but she does not seem to have remained in prison for long. Much less fortunate was Yevgeni Rodoslavov, from Odessa. He was only eighteen when arrested. It seems that he had done no more than take a leading part in the organization of local Baptist youth work. His trial took place in a typical atmosphere of hysteria. Young sympathizers standing outside the court were beaten up without any intervention from the police. Rodoslavov was given a sentence of incredible severity – five years in a prison camp, followed by five years in exile. Others tried with him received similar or lesser sentences.

Lyubov Lozinskaya (born 1950) was arrested in Tula on 3 February 1971. She was sentenced to one and a half years. Vladimir Bytin, born 1951, of Bryansk Region, was arrested in December 1969 and sentenced to one year.

The news filtering through about prison-camp conditions gives no ground for increased optimism. Ivan Afonin died in the Komsomolsky Camp, Tula, on 22 November 1969. He had apparently been forced to work when seriously ill, as the leader of the reform movement, Georgi Vins, also had been. Afonin had been doing a three-year sentence since March 1967. He was 43.

Alexi Iskovskikh, an old man of 70, sentenced in the Moscow Region in August 1968 to three years, died in a camp in January 1971. Pavel Zakharov died on 1 July 1971, in Pavlodar. His health had been exhausted by more than one imprisonment. His wife had already died in 1969, and today four orphaned children remain. Mrs Lidia Vins, mother of Georgi, was arrested in December 1970. She was sentenced in March to three years, and her friends doubt whether she will survive. She is so ill that she has to be physically led out to work. During her trial also, she had to be assisted into the dock. Early in 1972 she sent a note from prison to her relatives saying that if they mention "God" in their letters to her, the authorities will withhold the leters. Latest news is that she is now in the prison hospital.

In March 1969 a document was compiled by the so-called "Union of Christian Baptist Mothers", an impressive new organization allied to the reformers. This was an appeal to Mr Brezhnev and other Soviet officials, agencies and newspapers, backed by forty pages of signatures – 1,453 of them! – collected from 42 different towns and villages and from seven republics. The Ukraine is particularly strongly represented. The collection of signatures itself is a miracle of administration, considering the hostile conditions under which it was compiled. It gives strong evidence of resilience in the face of unwavering persecution. The writers give notice of the further deterioration of the situation in 1968. They mention

64 new arrests, affecting about 200 children – some of whom have even been thrown into prison with parents.

There are several individual contributions to the document. One of these comes from Nadezhda Sloboda and her husband Ivan, from the village of Dubravy, Belorussia. In February 1966 their two eldest daughters were taken away from them to a state boarding school because they were being brought up as Christians. Conditions there had seriously affected the children's health, and in January 1968 they ran away to return to their own home. After an unsuccessful attempt by the police to recover them from home, they were abducted from the local school and taken back to the boarding school.

The compilers of the mother's document add a sequel to this. Nadezhda Sloboda was sentenced on 11 December 1968 to four years in prison. The children were granted permission to go home for their Christmas holidays but when they arrived they found no mother there. The latest news of this family is that the other three small children have also been removed from their father and all five placed in different institutions. The family also had its radio set confiscated, because they had been listening to Christian programmes broadcast from outside the USSR.

Mention is made in the document of the new law on marriage and the family which came into operation on 1 October 1968, one directive of which is that parents should bring their children up in the spirit of the "Moral Code of a Builder of Communism" – that is, as atheists. This rendered easier the removal of children from religious parents, although, as we have seen, this had already been happening. It is perhaps significant that the atheist monthly "Science and Religion" (*Nauka i Religia*) in its issue of July 1971 published an article on orphanages and stated that the great majority of children in such institutions today were not without parents, but had in fact been removed from them for various reasons. Religion is not actually quoted as a major reason, but the writer does go on to speak about a specific case (here concerning the "True Orthodox" sect).

Another allegation comes from Mrs N. Rudich from the village of Borovitsa in the Ukraine. She describes how her son was consistently victimized by his teacher, until some of his classmates actualy tried, unsuccessfully, to throw him under a moving tractor. The boy was severely shocked, but the doctor diagnosed "a bad cold and catarrh" and consigned him to psychological tests.

At the same time as new arrests were made, some prisoners were released. By the end of 1969, no less than eighty had regained their freedom, including most of the leaders who had been imprisoned in 1966. It was a highly precarious liberty; nevertheless, at least for a short time, the best men in the reform movement were free to negotiate with the leaders of the All-Union Council for a reconciliation. As soon as they were free and fit again, the reform leaders gave this high priority. Activity along these lines had in fact continued in some form from the time of the official Baptist congress in 1966, though it had obviously not been representative on the side of the reformers, since their leaders were in prison.

The All-Union Council did, however, set up a Unity Commission and there is every evidence that it took its task of finding a solution very seriously. Some even said that it treated the reformers with too much consideration and tried to delve dispassionately into the problem, instead of accepting the official line laid down uncritically. This is revealed in the report by the Commission's secretary at the All-Union Council's Congress in December 1969 (published in the "Fraternal Messenger" No. 2, 1970). The fact that the secretary reproved those who regarded the Commission as a "neutral arm" instead of an organ of the AUCECB leads one to question how effective this Commission could be.

Meetings between the All-Union Council and the reformers took place on 19 April and 17 May 1969. As it later transpired, Sergei Golev, one of the most revered leaders of the reform movement, was negotiating under severe duress. He had only recently been released from prison (as had two others at the meetings), but on 3 April a new investigation had opened against him. He may well have been under threat to find a solution to the problem.

It seems that relations between the two sides were very friendly at the first session. Each side put forward its case and it seems that some verbal concessions at least were made from the official side.

Unfortunately, these relations soured in the interval between the two meetings. Mutual recriminations were made about breaking the agreement of silence on what had been discussed at the first meeting. The reformers accused the All-Union Council of withdrawing its previous readiness to repent publicly of its promulgation of the new line in 1960. We can do no more than speculate on whether or not state pressure was brought to bear on the All-Union Council in the intervening month. At any rate the meeting dissolved without concrete agreement. The All-Union Council appeared to show less pessimism about the situation, and produced a draft text of agreement which they said they would sign. The reformers stated that they would need to consult with their brethren about the agreement.

Two months later Golev was arrested and quickly sentenced to three years in a strict regime camp – already an old man, he was so weak that he had to be helped into the dock during his trial. Recent documents refer regularly to the fears of his friends that he might not survive this imprisonment.

Despite this, attempts at a reconciliation continued. Further consultations took place on 29 October and 4 December. Representatives of the All-Union Council expressed willingness to repent publicly for having adopted the controversial *New Statutes* of 1960, but only if the reformers would repent of sins on their side, which the latter refused to do. The All-Union Council put forward another draft agreement, which the reformers found quite unacceptable. Later, in February 1970, the reformers accused the official Baptists of circulating this draft as an agreed "Joint Declaration" and deceiving many churches. Such an action, the reformers said, showed that the official body was still capable of betraying its flock, just as in 1960.

These meetings virtually marked the end of negotiations between the two sides. The official Baptists in their publication continue to express a readiness to accept the "separated brethren" back into fellowship, but the reformers seem to have become steadily harder in their attitude. In December 1970 they wrote a lengthy diatribe on the AUCECB, calling on its leaders to repent and the people to come over to their side.

In November 1969 the Council of Baptist Prisoners' Relatives organized its first All-Union Congress at an unknown location. Various texts were produced at that meeting, including a further prisoner list of 176 names. This list confirmed that several reformers had been released during the year and the total number then in prison had fallen below the 200-mark for the first time in several years. However, as the participants of the congress pointed out, recent trends were not encouraging and a number of new names had been added during the year.

The congress also issued an appeal "To All Christian Churches: To All Christians of the World," which gave some general reflections on the past century of Russian Baptist history. Its calm and reasoned tone, with a factual account of sufferings past and present, makes a strong contrast to an article in *Izvestia* by Vladimir Kuroyedov, head of the government Council on Religious Affairs, shortly before the congress convened. The 62 signatories of this appeal repudiated his inflammatory acusations of anti-Soviet activity with immense restraint and dignity.

In December 1969 there were two further events of significance: a conference held by the reformers on 6 December at Tula, and a triennial All-Union Congress in Moscow from 9-11 December.

The former was a unique occasion. It was the first time ever that the state authorities had given permission for the reformers to meet officially. Even though the permission was given only three days before the conference opened, 120 delegates assembled, representing 47 different areas of the Soviet Union.

Gennadi Kryuchkov was elected chairman of the meeting and reported on the activity of the Council of ECB Churches (as the reformers now call themselves) since 1966. He said that some of the leaders had been invited to attend the imminent All-Union Congres in Moscow, but the meeting decided unanimously that this should be declined, since they were expressly forbidden the right to speak or vote.

Representatives of six registered congregations attended the meeting, which went on at its evening session to discuss the whole issue of registration. It was decided to issue a call to all congregations that they should apply or re-apply for registration, using a form of application which was now in operation.

Obviously those present at the Tula meeting must have

had high hopes that at last the attitude of the authorities was going to change towards them. If they could now start to register their congregations, which up to now the state had consistently refused, they would feel that the discrimination against them was lessening and they might be able to look forward to a more normal religious life in the future. They probably felt, too, that with such a turn of events, it would be easier to negotiate with the All-Union Council over the question of unity.

In a mood of some buoyancy, therefore, they penned a letter to Mr Kosygin requesting permission for all eight legally-elected members of the Council of Churches to be relieved from the obligation to do secular work (to which, of course, registered pastors under the All-Union Council had always been entitled).

This new mood of confidence was to be short-lived. Many congregations under the Council of Churches had long been seeking registration, but nevertheless renewed their efforts as a result of the new directive from the meeting. Believers at Krivoi Rog reported that they had put in an application on 4 January 1970, but the local police reacted by coming and breaking up their meeting by force. Several of them were heavily fined for having met for worship.

Much more serious was a whole new wave of arrests in various parts of the Soviet Union (obviously representing a concerted policy), affecting some of the top leaders of the Council of Churches. Georgi Vins, having been free for only a few months, was arrested yet again. On 21 January 1970, he was sentenced to a year's forced labour for not being gainfully employed – a direct rebuff to his request to serve full-time as a pastor. This did not actualy entail removal to prison, but he was obliged to remain at a certain place of work in his home town of Kiev. Before the year was up, however, Vins informed the authorities that this state of affairs was impossible and that he should be working entirely for the church. He was twice summoned to the police in August, although he did not appear. No further details are known at the moment, beyond the fact that he is still severely threatened by the authorities.

Mikhail Khorev, who had taken a prominent part in the Tula consultation in December and who had been at liberty for less than a year after his previous sentence, was arrested at Kishinev less than two weeks after the meeting. He was now partially blind. His wife was taken seriously ill at the same time and had to go to a hospital, leaving three children under eight at home unattended. He was tried in July 1970. His wife was not informed of the place of the trial and was forced to scour the town for hours in the rain before locating it. She was not allowed to speak to her husband and he was given no rest or food during the whole day of the trial. Khorev was sentenced to three years strict regime.

The question arises: what was the purpose of the authorities in allowing the Tula consultation, if it was to be immediately followed by a new wave of repressions? The answer seems to be that the release of most of the leaders in 1969 confronted the authorities with a new problem: the threat of renewed activity among the reformers, which might result in a new wave of uncontrolled evangelism up and down the country. The most likely explanation of what happened is that the authorities wanted to isolate the most active leaders of the continuing movement by allowing them to convene; this would also provide the opportunity of discovering what were their latest attitudes over a number of questions. If they had been hoping that the representatives at the consultation would make a call for the reform of Soviet law and thus lay themselves open to attack, they were disappointed, but the state stepped in nevertheless.

The triennial congress of the All-Union Council from 9-11 December 1969 was a different affair altogether. It was a big public – indeed international – occasion, with several foreign guests taking a prominent part. Dr Ronald Goulding, London representative of the Baptist World Alliance, was one of them and upon his return he wrote that an overwhelming desire for reunion had been displayed by the delegates and that this had become the dominant theme of the congress. The long summary of the proceedings as printed in the "Fraternal Messenger" (No. 2, 1970) bears this out.

The late Alexander Karev, Secretary of the Council, reported at great length and in a tone of optimism about the advances which had been made in a whole range of areas since the last congress three years before: the theological correspondence course, the printing of the Bible and hymn book, growth in membership (by at least 13,000 in the past three years, excluding the return of 3,000 'schismatics", as he called them, and 2,250 Pentecostals who had joined the Union).

Although some criticism of the All-Union Council was expressed (particularly for spending too much time on foreign visits and not enough on domestic ones), the general tone – at least as reported in the Council's own organ – was one of satisfaction. Rather bitter criticism of the reformers was expressed by some. S. T. Timchenko, vice-president of the Council, gave the main speech on unity. While suggesting that the activities of the "schismatics" were a reproach to the brotherhood, he affirmed that the promulgation of the *Letter of Instructions* and the *New Statutes* in 1960 had been a mistake which had since been rectified.

Pastor Timchenko sharply repudiated the action of the Council of Prisoners' Relatives after their November congress in spreading what he called "false information" to organizations outside the Soviet Union, containing "rumours about persecution of the church and about the alleged physical liquidation of believers." (It should be noted that even Soviet atheists have tacitly admitted the factual accuracy of such documents in the past.) He ended by paying tribute to the personal conduct of the leaders of the reform movement, including Kryuchkov and Vins, at the unity meetings in October and December.

A Note About Statistics

Alexander Karev ("Fraternal Messenger", no. 3-4, 1954, p. 91) once said, "We have as many as 5,400 congregations, each of which consists of not less than twenty members, and 512,000 believers who have been baptized for their faith. But if one takes the members of believers' families and other people close to our brotherhood, then the total number of such can be reckoned at three million."

Evidence of successful evangelism since 1954 suggests a rise in membership, yet official statistics subsequently dropped drastically. F. Fedorenko, in *Sects, Their Faith and Practice* (1965), gave the number of communities as "about 2,000" and membership as "more than 200,000". Karev, at the 1966 congress, gave the total strength as no more than 500,000, with baptized members composing no more than half this number.

This certainly indicates that some congregations have disbanded, but equally certainly some have seceded and now operate unofficially. In Latvia 14 out of 82 congregations were disbanded between 1960 and 1963. Absolute estimates of numbers of reform Baptists have been given officially as five or eight per cent, but these are ambiguous: per cent of what? An absolute figure has been given of 15,000, but this is certainly an underestimate. One representative of a Western mission with close connections among the reform Baptists gives the figure of "more than 1,000" for their congregations.

The reform Baptists themselves at one point stated that two-thirds of Baptist congregations were unregistered. This does not necessarily mean that they all support the reformers, but undoubtedly many of them do. The fact that this group is attacked in the Soviet press more systematically than any other suggests that their numbers are not insignificant.

An official newspaper cites one of the few cases for which we have actual statistics: that of the Brest congregation which was joined with another some distance away. Out of 380 believers only about 100 went to the other church. The rest began to organize illegal meetings in Brest. In this specific case almost three-quarters of a single congregation supported the reformers.

III

THE LIFE OF A YOUNG CHRISTIAN

by XENIA HOWARD-JOHNSTON

AIDA SKRIPNIKOVA was born in 1941. She learnt the sorrow of a suffering people young, for her father was shot as a pacifist while she was an infant.

Aida's mother tried to give her a Christian upbringing from the first. Aida says she did not think about religion very much when young, but independence of mind this upbringing certainly gave her. Even as a fourteen-year-old she demonstrated quite exceptional courage for a young Soviet person. At the time of the Pasternak affair (1958), when the novel *Dr. Zhivago* was violently attacked by the Soviet authorities, Aida wrote to *Pravda* what the authorities termed an "anti-Soviet" letter, in which she protested at the way Pasternak was condemned before those accusing him had even read his novel.

In her late teens she was much influenced by the faith of her brother. Already in August 1961, Aida was searching for a personal faith in Jesus Christ: she approached a young Englishman, Stuart Robertson (then visiting Leningrad) after the service at the Leningrad Baptist Church and asked him many questions about the Christian faith. Under this influence and others, Aida became a Christian later that year: her beloved brother had died and in her trouble she found renewed strength and a new life in the family of Christ. The "awakening" within the ECB Church, and the establishment of a new independent organization touched Aida too. "Faith was growing weak", she said, "and suddenly there came an awakening. What I saw was quite miraculous. I saw the dead rising again – the spiritually dead, the weak proved capable of great feats. Once I was attracted by impressive external greatness, but then I came to know the greatness of humility and patience, the kind of greatness of the Church's struggle.

This revival quickened my spirit, too, and from that time onwards I have not been able to remain uninvolved."

That year (1961) on New Year's Eve, she acted upon her newly found faith by courageously standing up in public, in the Nevsky Prospekt, and distributing postcards on which she had written a poem of her own composition. The postcard was of a picture in the Hermitage Museum by Claude-Lorraine, representing a harbour at sunrise (chosen, perhaps, as a symbol of the spiritual sunrise which she had discovered) and the poem on it expressed Aida's awareness of life's shortness, of its pain and grief, and the need to search for and find God before we die. The death of her brother must surely have made her particularly conscious of the end of life at this time.

HAPPY NEW YEAR! 1962

A New Year Wish

Our years fly past
One after the other, unnoticed.
Grief and sadness disappear,
They are carried away by life.
This world, the earth, is so transient
Everything in it comes to an end.
Life is important. Don't be happy-go-lucky!
What answer will you give your Creator?
What awaits you, my friend, beyond the grave?
Answer this question, while light remains,
Perhaps tomorrow, before God
You will appear to give an answer for everything.
Think deeply about this,
For you are not on this earth to eternity.
Perhaps tomorrow, you will break
For ever your links with this world!
SEEK GOD WHILE HE IS TO BE FOUND!

This slender, pale, brown-eyed girl standing on a street corner on a freezing cold night in Leningrad may not have presented a dramatic picture, but her action started a train of events which is still evolving. Neither Russia nor the world will forget her.

For distributing this poem in the street, Aida was arrested. In April 1962 she was tried by a Comrades' Court, which informed her that she must no longer live in Leningrad and that she was to lose her job as a laboratory assistant and be transferred to work on a building site. The court, it appears from the transcript of Aida's trial in 1968, took three years before it eventually carried out its decision. From 1962 onwards she was frequently slandered in the Soviet press: according to a Baptist document dated 15 August 1967[1] this continued for five years. For example, on 4 June 1962 an article entitled "Don't be a corpse among the living" appeared in *Smena* (see pp. 29–34), to which Aida wrote a powerful answer in September 1962 (see pp. 35–44), but her article was of course not published. In addition she was attacked in *Izvestia* and *Evening Leningrad*[2] in 1964. Even books referred to her. V. R. Bukin in *Psychology of Believers and Atheist Education* (published in 1969, but of course written earlier) said that "experienced Baptists" exploited her "desire to be popular" and made her active on their behalf (accusations which her trial show not to have been true).

With a campaign mounting against her Aida lost her residence permit for Leningrad and could no longer live in her home town.

One girl's action in circulating a defence of the Christian faith to friends may not seem of great significance. Yet Aida was in the very forefront of the *samizdat* (self-publishing) movement. Her friends were impressed with what she wrote. Some so much that they made copies of the article which they passed on to other friends. These, in their turn, made more copies. The circle widened. Curiosity about the girl attacked in the press grew. People began to ask for her article. It was a remarkable defence of the Christian faith by any standards—not least from a young girl conscious of challenging the whole weight of the atheist system by sending it

1. Rosemary Harris and Xenia Howard-Johnston (eds.) *Christian Appeals from Russia,* London 1969, p. 57.
2. "*Possev,* Frankfurt, No. 9, 1968, p. 59: the title of the *Izvestia* article was 'Pirates from the prayer house', and the article in *Evening Leningrad* was entitled 'Obscurantist baseness'. In addition *Smena* published another article in 1964, entitled 'In the meshes of religious fanatics'."
3. *Christian Appeals from Russia,* p. 58.

around. A new form of literary circulation was born. Other Soviet people used similar methods for distributing unpublished literature, so that *samizdat* has now become a nationwide phenomenon. But the Christians –and none more actively than the teen-aged Aida – were there from the very beginning.

This was a fulfilment of her love for God and her country, not a betrayal. At her trial in 1968, she expressed the great love she bore for her country and longed to see an end to persecution:

> "Our country could be the most beautiful country in the world were there no persecution."

In her concern for those suffering for their faith in the USSR, she took upon herself the dangerous and difficult task of informing the outside world of what was happening to the ECB Church. As well as helping to circulate the reform Baptist *samizdat* publications, *Herald of Salvation* and *Fraternal Leaflet* within the USSR, she began building up contacts with foreigners and trying to hand on to them transcripts of the trials of Christians and the lists of Baptist prisoners, drawn up by a group of their wives, as well as other appeals and letters written by Russian ECB Christians in which they described their plight. Those abroad must know what was happening, she felt, and to this end she risked her own well-being.

Through her we discover a little of that "miracle" of which she spoke at her trial in 1968:

> "What is happening in the life of our church is a miracle. In the twentieth century when atheists are shouting about the extinguishing of faith, a fire like this suddenly flares up. And I wanted everybody to know about this miracle of awakening."

As part of her work of distributing the reform Baptists' *samizdat* literature and collecting material on trials, imprisonments and other forms of persecution for sending abroad, Aida went to stay with her sister in the Ukraine in early 1964, where she was much impressed by the boldness of Christians. She returned in the spring of that year only to find that the police were on the look-out for her, waiting at the bus and train terminals in Leningrad. Nevertheless, Aida managed to outwit the police and got into Leningrad unobserved.

Before leaving for the Ukraine she had given up her job, and on her return had great difficulty in finding work. She eventually managed to find a job at a milk-bottling centre. Before going south to the Ukraine she had lost her residence permit for Leningrad as well as her job; all her efforts to get re-registered in Leningrad failed.

Meanwhile the police were continuing to look for Aida: they searched the homes of various Christians at midnight and in the early morning; they questioned others about her and in 1965 she was eventually arrested at a prayer-meeting held in a forest (since the group had not been able to obtain registration). This is how Marfa Akimovna Skurlova, a witness at Aida's trial and a Christian friend, described Aida's arrest and subsequent trial:

> "We had a meeting in the woods, the police arrived and began chasing us off. They pushed and grabbed us by the hair. They took away several people: some they fined. Aida was arrested and brought to trial. . . . And what a trial they organized. It wasn't a good court. She was brought to some factory; they shouted and made a noise; Aida wasn't even given a chance to speak."

At this trial she was sentenced to one year in prison.

After her release at the end of 1966, she again had great difficulty in finding work, nor was she allowed to live in Leningrad, but registered in Volkhovstroye, where she moved into a friend's room in a communal flat on 9 April 1967. After being taken on as an employee at a printing works, where train timetables and forms were printed, she was dismissed on 21 April 1967, after her name had been taken down by the police for attending a prayer meeting. She considered, at her trial, justifiably, that it was because of her faith that she was dismissed. Both a factory and a home for the disabled then refused to employ her because she was a Christian.

Sometime in these years Aida was also forcibly detained in a psychiatric clinic, but she was found to be completely normal and was released.

It was about the time of her dismissal from the printing works, that is in the spring of 1967, that persecution of evangelical believers in Leningrad became more severe: Christians were not allowed to meet in private, their homes were searched, many of them were summoned to the Procurator's office for questioning, some were arrested and others fined.

In May 1967 the police began searching for Aida and questioning those who knew her in an attempt to build up a case against her. They withdrew her residence permit for Volkhovstroye in July or August 1967 so that they could accuse her of residing illegally in the communal flat. This is how a document written on 15 August 1967[3] described Aida's plight:

> "For nearly six months she has not been able to show herself at home. The police have been visiting several believers' homes and declaring that they were searching for Aida Skripnikova. The neighbours are required to watch her flat. At the present time a new court case is in preparation against her."

Nearly a year elapsed from the start of the search and enquiry into Aida's activities in the spring of 1967 and her eventual arrest on 12 April 1968. The day before her arrest she was followed after she had been at a service and the next day, from 7 a.m. until 9.30 p.m., her room was meticulously searched by the police and Aida found herself under arrest. Transcripts of trials of reform Baptists, a list of prisoners, various appeals to Brezhnev and to the UN were confiscated, as well as many issues of *Herald of Salvation*, *Fraternal Leaflet* and a copy of the Bible, her notebook, personal letters and photographs. The fact that she possessed such documents and had tried to get many of them abroad was used as evidence against her: for it was claimed by the prosecution that these documents contained "deliberately false statements, slandering the Soviet state and socialist order" (Article 190/1 of the RSFSR Criminal Code).

Perhaps the most remarkable feature of Aida's trial, which opened on 11 July 1968, is not how she was harassed and barred from fighting the case on the essential issue of whether or not there is religious persecution in the USSR; it is the unanimous and courageous testimony from all the witnesses to Aida's utter integrity of character. Here was a person who impressed believers and non-believers by being herself, by being seized with a passionate loyalty to God, which gave people a new perspective on the over-exploited issue of "patriotism". Christians and atheists, Soviet and foreign, had much to learn from Aida. Were she never to utter another syllable, she would still have made an important contribution to the development of Soviet society. Aida forcefully defended herself (without the help of a defence lawyer) at her trial with the argument that none of the facts contained in the reform Baptist documents was false and that they therefore could not be termed slander. Nor did these documents or her attempts to get them abroad harm the Soviet state and social order. Russian Christians, she claimed, are law-abiding citizens, not opposed to the Soviet state and social order; they are tried, harassed and fined, not for breaking the law, but for their faith.

To Aida, the article on freedom of worship in the Constitution, despite its ban on "religious propaganda", implied, by guaranteeing freedom of conscience, the freedom for a Christian to *confess* his faith, that is to teach children about the Christian faith and to engage in missionary activity. For belief and the expression in words and action of this belief could not be separated. If this article in the Constitution were interpreted, as it is officially in the USSR, as forbidding Christians to express their faith in word and action outside the walls of the building alloted to a registered Christian community by the state, then such a law could not be observed by a Christian: for as Aida said in her defence speech ". . . believers cannot promise to fulfil a law which forbids them to talk about God and forbids parents to bring up their children in the faith. For all their loyalty to the authorities, believers will not subscribe to such a law. No Christian mother or father will accept a law which orders them to bring up their children as atheists."

Despite her vigorous and well-argued defence, Aida was sentenced on 15 July to three years of imprisonment.

The experience of prison did not lead Aida to despair and hopelessness. She knew from personal experience the truth of the following words, contained in the reform Baptists' *Easter Greeting* of 13 March 1969, addressed to persecuted Russian Christians:

"Today HE walks through the dark, damp prison cells, the labour camps surrounded by barbed wire, through the cold regions of the north – the places of exile . . . He visits the families of prisoners, He visits the persecuted Church as the CONQUEROR, 'Be of good courage! I have overcome the world!' "

So deep was Aida's spiritual quality, so outgoing the love which she radiated, that even those among her fellow-prisoners who had no sympathy with the Christian faith were moved to help her. When the prison authorities tried to confiscate her Bible, they would all join in a conspiracy to conceal it. Between her and her fellows there was a constant unruffled atmosphere of love and trust.

The authorities were obviously embarrassed at the stream of food-parcels, letters and cards which arrived from abroad. On one occasion they showed her the contents of a parcel, but refused to allow her to touch it. She later said that the knowledge that such friends were praying for her and trying to help her gave her more sustenance than the richest food-parcel she could have imagined.

In a private letter dated 21 January 1970, Aida thanked God for "this road" along which she had been led, for it had been a blessing and, by walking along it, she had learnt much and experienced the love of God. Because her happiness did not depend on external circumstances, it could not be destroyed. Although many days during her imprisonment had been very hard to bear, although she missed her freedom, her home and friends, she never regretted her action in trying to send abroad information about persecution of Christians in the USSR, nor could she have rejected the command of God to do this work for the sake of an easier life, for without God life, to her, was meaningless. As she said at the end of her final speech at the trial:

> "I'm not a heroine. I love freedom and would very much like to be free now with my family and friends. But I can't buy freedom at any price; I don't want to act against my conscience. I love freedom, but what good is freedom to me if I can't call God my Father? . . . The knowledge that my soul and thoughts are free encourages and strengthens me."

On 12 April 1971, Aida was released from prison: her face had grown thinner during those three years, but it was alight with the Life of Christ who had granted her His grace and presence.

IV

DON'T BE A CORPSE AMONG THE LIVING

by V. I. KUZIN[1]

Aida,

I HAVE received your letter and tracts entitled *"Before It Is Too Late"* and *"Crime Against The Law of Religious Freedom"* which you sent me in answer to my article, *"The Christian Fishers' Empty Nets."*

Your letter demands of me, an atheist journalist, to repent and stop blaspheming God. You have exhorted me to "believe on the Lord Jesus Christ." In the name of your God, you offer me "salvation" if I will repent. I am really touched by your concern, but I have to disappoint you. My "sinful soul" is very healthy and without danger. The word "soul" to an atheist indicates nothing more than the brain, "a possibility to think and feel," according to Pavlov, and nothing else. Believe me, I would have never given publicity to our letters or talks if the contents had been only of a personal nature. Our disagreement, however, is a controversy between two beliefs and two moral codes which are poles apart. Our dispute is about a *goal* and a *purpose* in life and if to believe in God is dangerous or good for a man or woman. It is a dispute about your personal destiny, Aida. *That is the reason why I cannot be quiet.*

I answer you and all those cowards who are hiding behind your back – those Baptist fanatics you call your "friends" (I call them your enemies – Lvov, Lukinov, Filipov, Akaki, Mikhailov, Semenova, Khorev, Grineva, and Serbakova). These young people, your so-called "brothers and sisters in Christ", have recently been seized by an insatiable desire for prayer-meetings organized in private flats and have been guilty of spreading evangelical literature.

What does all this mean? Nobody forbids you to believe in God. You have your own prayer house in Moscow and your

1. The text of this article appears to be incomplete, since some passages referred to by Aida in her reply are not included.

own religious paper printed there. Why then this hostility? In your letters to me you state that the reason for your zealous witness to your "Redeemer" is that He is coming soon and that the great judgment day is ahead, so that one has to hurry up and "get saved" and get ready to meet God. (Your concern for me is touching!!)

Let us be sincere, Aida. You and all the others know very well that the issue does not concern the Biblical doctrine of the second-coming of Christ, but has arisen because there is a crisis among the Baptists of the Soviet Union. In my article in *Smena* I stated that the ranks of the Baptists are getting smaller every year and that your "nets are empty." You have therefore to seek new forms and methods for getting new members. The fact that large groups of fanatics have arisen in your Baptist church is a sign that here is a big Baptist crisis. And you, Aida, have taken active part in the hostile acts of these fanatic groups against the Soviet Union, although there is for you complete religious freedom.

I feel very sad for you, because in spite of all this religious nonsense you are not too far gone yet that you cannot recover yourself. You are a creature of circumstances because you have been brought up in a Baptist environment. You are lost in a labyrinth. I am sorry for you because the *human being* in you is dying. A "human being" is the wonder of the earth and all other wonders belong to him. A "human being" is a wonderful thing. Life is given only once and you ought to live so as not to have regrets about the wasted years.

According to the programme of the Communist Party, the human being should be educated to be an individual who has fully and harmoniously developed. Lenin spoke of such a human being in The Party's Third Congress:

> *"Only by enriching one's experience through a complete knowledge of the riches that have formed humanity can one become a Communist."*

Karl Marx has described the human being's moral features in his remarkable answer to the questions his daughter had written. The founder of Communism has clearly pointed out the human being's high ideal and moral principle in his book, *Our Life Codex.* Is this simple, deep, humanism, which is the only true wisdom, also your life's codex? If not, then the human being in you is dying. I can hear you answer, "To believe in the Lord Jesus Christ, our Redeemer, does not ruin a human being. This belief makes a human being clean, as he is born again. God is love."

Let us briefly see things clearly. Our moral appearance is judged by the *purpose* of our life. What purpose do you Baptists have? You, Aida, preach that according to the holy gospel the goal of life is "to be redeemed by Christ and live for Him while here on earth and then to be saved from eternal damnation."

Briefly, what you most fear in this world is death and what you most want is "eternal life" and personal salvation by grace. This is the only reason, Aida, why you believe in Christ . . .

"He that believeth on the Son hath everlasting life, and he that believeth not the Son shall not see life; but the wrath of God abideth on him" (John 3:26).

You Baptists believe in this statement in the gospel of John, even though the truth of it is very doubtful. Fear and ignorance dictate the goal of your life. No wonder our Communist young people call you "living corpses" and "songsters about life after death"! These are hard words for you to hear, but it is true. You sing about being pilgrims and strangers because *heaven is your goal*. Baptists see the meaning of life in getting themselves well prepared for the after-life. Is not this the philosophy of those who are living, but in reality are dead? Your Baptist corpses are cruel and selfish because you yourselves are saved while others are lost. "All others are lost (hurrah!). We are secure."

We atheists are not against eternal life, but it must exist here, on earth, not in a world beyond. Immortality consists for us not, as religion promises, in sitting idly in some sort of Elysian field, munching sticky buns and unconcernedly watching the larger part of humanity suffer agony in fiery Gehenna. *We believe man achieves immortality through his work. He is eternal through what he performs for the happiness of all humanity.*

Will Pushkin's or Tolstoy's, or Tchaikovsky's, or Beethoven's work ever die? Or the deeds of Gagarin and Titov? Are not the deed of great physicians immortal? All these are living today through their works. The goal of our generation is to build Communism and live under it. There exists no goal more noble or more wonderful than this. Aida, do you find this to be the goal which inspires your "brothers and sisters in Christ?" Are you ready to strike for this goal in order to be immortal, or are you training yourself to be an idler in God's heaven?

We look upon our goal also to be the educating of our children, so that the next generation will follow after our ideals. Young people will be proud and disciplined and will lift high the Communist banner. With this wonderful goal in view, we do not spare our strength and energy and if necessary we give our lives. We do not fear death. We do not need to invent gods, because our work is eternal. We are living in it and will do so forever.

Every sensible person in our twentieth century understands that your mysterious life-after-death, compared to our Communist earthly experience, is a worthless one. You inherited these beliefs from your forefathers who were ignorant people. They may be forgiven, but you who live in this intelligent age ought to be ashamed of your ignorance. You young Baptist girls and young women ought not to be proud of your beliefs and your "Saviour," but instead you should be ashamed of believing such nonsensical biblical teachings. You Baptist young people ought to be ashamed of your egotism and moral behaviour. Your Christian life is an easy one, as you do not need to work hard to gain your "eternal life." It is "by grace" and not by striving or good works. You are lazy. You do not need our Communist philosophy. It is unusual that any of you studies. You are not striving to reach the heights of culture. You Baptists look upon the cinema and the reading of worldly books as sin. In fact, to you it is not necessary to be a person of morals. The only thing necessary is to "have faith in Christ." One of your favourite authors writes:

"When you stand before the great white throne of Judgment, the one big question that will be asked you will be: 'What did you do with My beloved Son here on earth? Did you receive Him or reject Him?' Your moral living will be of no avail."

So you see that it is not forbidden to a Christian to kill, steal, live an immoral life, or even betray his Fatherland. Your Baptist gospel declared, "Immediately a person receives Christ, his sin disappears and he becomes a new creation in

Christ Jesus" (II Corinthians 5:17).

Why, Aida, has not the Christian religion during its 2000 years' existence raised moral standards and destroyed all evil? Why has not your gospel been able to banish from the earth the inhuman exploitation of individual against individual? We Communists, who are atheists, have done this very thing by revolution. Only under Communism, for instance, have women achieved their human rights. And I could ask you many other questions, but you will only reply, "It so pleased God." Of course you know, Aida, you have no answers to my logic. The reason is simple: religion has never and never can teach people things that are good, because religion is inhuman and without morals. In your Bible we read that God sent fire to burn the whole population of Sodom and Gomorrah, allowing only Lot and his two daughters to escape. The Bible is full of such descriptions of God's immoral deeds.

Christ, who supposedly came into this world to create order, preached cruelty. When he sent his disciples to different places, he gave them instructions on how to behave in case they were not received: "But I say unto you that it shall be more tolerable in that day for Sodom than for that city" (Luke 10:12). Christ presents Himself as being "meek and lowly in heart," but threatens all his enemies with severe punishment on the great judgment day. Where do you find the patience and love that he preaches?

We atheists do not mock God or Christ because one can only mock that which exists; it is impossible to mock that which does not exist. We Communists have always been against religion because its teaching harms people and it has destroyed you, Aida.

The most important reason why the Baptist way is an enemy to the country is because it is a false way and has a false principle of life. The Bible is false and a compendium of legends. You, Aida, have lost the elementary ideas of the law of human life. You try to oppose that which is holy to every Soviet citizen – freedom of conscience. Lenin's decree is freedom of conscience for every individual. The church and the state must be separated from each other. The freedom of conscience that they claim to have in the United States of America is more in favour with you Baptists. Atheists and unbelievers who do not believe in Jesus Christ there are cast into prison. Even here in Russia, you Baptists are against our having freedom to propagate our anti-god message. You will never succeed. Our people will never give away that which they have obtained. Our Communist workers in the factory of Nogina, in Narvskaya, have already warned you Baptists that they are going to sentence Semenova, Serbakova, and *yourself* to heavy imprisonment.

The Soviet laws apply to both believers and unbelievers alike; everyone has to keep them. It is a pity that neither you nor your "brothers and sisters in Christ" have done so. You continue with your enmity against the community. You continue with your role as "fishers for Christ," but your nets are empty, as they always have been. You continue your propaganda against us in order that you may occupy a high position in your Baptist church.

Religion has already made you a young invalid, Aida. It has already taken away from you many wonderful human qualities. Your gospel has turned you into a hypocrite. It has deprived you of the joy of youth. Your Baptist way has forced you to think only of death and heaven and has deprived you of culture and science which is the joy of the Communist youth. As a Christian, you remain ignorant and uncultured.

In closing, may I ask you with all earnestness, do you want to become a real Human Being? There are only two choices before you: either become a human being through accepting Communism or continue to be a slave of God. You must choose for yourself. Before you is a wonderful world in which to build, create, love, dream and venture. The true life is not that of being God's slave, but to be a real sovereign person, belonging to one's self. Ahead of you is the glory of fighting for immortality, gained with your own hand, through your own works and talents and not through prayers and psalm-singing to the glory of the mystical Jesus.

But you are on the other way, where your personality will perish. Before it is too late, consider the serious situation. Stop telling yourself and others lies. Your atheist friends are always ready to stretch out a helping hand toward you.

V

AIDA'S REPLY TO KUZIN[1]

by Aida Skripnikova

"For they all made us afraid, saying, Their hands shall be weakened from the work, and it shall not be done; but I strengthened my hands the more" (Nehemiah 6:9).

Let us talk about your article, Valen Ivanovich. Let us imagine that you and I have decided to compete against each other in a race. And suddenly you tie my legs together and rush towards the finishing post. "Hurray! I've won!" you cry triumphantly. "Untie my legs! Set me free! Then we'll see who'll win," I say. "Untie your legs? Set you free? But that would be an encroachment upon my freedom!" you answer.

What do you think an impartial judge would say, looking at this kind of a competition?

It is perhaps fear of defeat that makes you and those who think like you resort to dishonest methods, crude force.... If, according to you, people do not believe in God solely on account of their thought and their knowledge, why are you afraid that I, an ignoramus, should talk to clear-thinking people? Why put me in prison? Surely even our distant ancestors did not act in this way: their thinking, in your words, was so primitive that "unable to explain the laws of nature and society, they created heaven and hell". . . .

If *you* suddenly feel like spending some time amongst your close friends you do not have to be afraid that by doing this you will break the law. *You* can meet together at any time and do whatever you like: talk, read or sing. Why, then, can *we* not visit one another? What law forbids this? Why can we not pray or read the Bible whenever we want? We are

1. There are a few cuts in the present text at points where the original is illegible.

allowed to speak about God only in church. You would certainly not accept it if you were allowed to talk about plays only in a theatre or about books only in a library. In the same way we cannot be silent about what constitutes the whole meaning of our life – about Christ.

Wherever it is we meet, whether in church or in a private flat, we talk about Christ everywhere. You call our small friendly meetings illegal, but Christ sanctioned the right to meet; he said: "Where two or three are gathered together in my name, there am I in the midst."

"Call upon the Lord in all places." Christ did not say: pray only where you are allowed to. No! "in all places", and this means "pray even where it is not permitted"!

You organize large congresses, conferences, meetings, you have a great army of activists and yet you are afraid when a few people meet to pray to God. "No one forbids you to believe in God", you say today. I am sure that you will say the same tomorrow. Perhaps in a short time, to pray will be considered a terrible crime. Where is the guarantee that tomorrow you will not shut a church? Of course you can shut a church, but this cannot destroy the church of Christ. "For ye are the temple of the living God", says the Bible (2 Cor. 6:16).

"No one forbids you to believe in God." We believe, not because you generously give us permission; we would go on believing even if you were to forbid it. We are Christians not because "religious liberty" is inscribed in the constitution of the USSR, but because Christ died on Golgotha.

From the history of past centuries we know about the times of the Roman Caesars, when Christians were persecuted and destroyed; we know about the Inquisition, when the living Church of Christ was persecuted – a time when people were burnt at the stake and tortured. But now it is the twentieth century and we see how little it differs from past centuries: it is a century of prisons and deportations. Has the experience of history really not convinced you that there is no power which can wipe Christianity from the face of the earth? God said: "Behold, they shall arm themselves *against thee,* but not at my bidding: Whosoever shall arm himself against thee shall fall. No weapon that is formed against thee shall prosper" (Isaiah 54:15, 17).

You do not like it when we speak to people about God, about salvation. Why do we do this? Only so that you should not perish. The coming of Christ will certainly be soon, but many will pass into eternal life before Christ comes. We must not look on calmly as people choose the path which leads to destruction. Our duty is to show these people the true path.

With reference to your statement, "The more sinners you save, the wider you think the gates of heaven will open for you", I would like to ask you: where did you find such a statement in the Bible? Did Christ, when sending out his disciples to spread the good news, say to them: "the more sinners you save, the wider will the gates of heaven open for you"? And did the thief, crucified on the cross, save any sinners? He nonetheless heard the wonderful words: "Today shalt thou be with me in paradise"....

Something else is needed for personal salvation. What is it? The Bible gives a clear, comprehensive answer to this question: "He that believeth on the Son hath everlasting life" (John 3; 36.) For by grace are ye saved through faith; and that not of yourselves: it is the gift of God" (Eph. 2:8). Thus life is eternal, salvation is a gift and it is freely given to man. . . .

And then you do not like us distributing religious letters. Imagine that a fire has started and that you must warn people of the danger, wake them up. You would sound the alarm. But if there should be no alarm bell near at hand, you would grab hold of any old bucket, even one full of holes, and would begin hitting it. No one would blame you for using an old, useless bucket in those circumstances.

Allow us to publish a mass-circulation newspaper which could be bought in a kiosk, and I assure you we would not need to distribute religious letters.

If you do not like us holding prayer meetings in private flats, then allow us to study the Bible in church, allow us to hold small meetings of young people in church, allow us to meet in our church whenever we want to .

You are mistaken when you say that we have "recently been seized by an insatiable desire for prayer meetings organized in private flats". It is incorrect to say "recently".

When I was very small, people very often met in our flat to read the Bible and pray. They met despite the cruel persecution that could result (1947). They went on meeting even after the night when several people were arrested (1946-47). After spending eight to ten years in prison, these people again began meeting to read the Bible and pray. We also meet now, and you can do nothing about it.

No doubt you are now smiling to yourselves: 'Ah, but we've already done something!"

Maybe. But this was only because of our weakness.

When people spend the night in a forest, they light a great bonfire, not only in order to keep themselves warm, but also to protect themselves from wolves. Wolves will not approach a bonfire. They stand very close, viciously grinding their teeth, but will not approach the bonfire. But the flames burn lower and lower . . . the ring of people draws closer and closer together . . . they're already very close to it! Quick, throw on some wood. The fire blazes up with renewed strength and the wolves move away. Beside a bright flame they are not to be feared.

"What! stand by the flames?! In view of the whole pack?! Terrifying! I'm going to hide in the bushes!"

"Friend! In the bushes the wolves are far more dangerous. go to the fire! Quickly to the fire!"

One feels like saying to those who are afraid today: "To the fire, friends! Quickly to the fire!"

You state that we demand the baning of anti-religious propaganda produced by atheist journalists. We have never demanded this. On the contrary, we would not agree if we were given complete freedom and you were forbidden to carry on anti-religious propaganda. We would be against this, firstly because it would be dishonest, secondly because when anti-religious propaganda is being carried on, it is easier for us to show up the hollowness of your arguments.

Indeed, what can you set against reality and the truth? At the moment you have recourse to lies and slander, you distort and juggle the facts (this by itself is clear proof that the truth cannot be on your side). It is therefore quite understandable that you are afraid of giving us freedom.

It is absurd to announce that if believers were to be given freedom, then this would be an infringement of the workers' freedom of conscience. How could it constitute such an infringement if a Christian periodical, such as *The Young Christian* or *Joyful News*, were to lie beside *Komsomol Truth* in a kiosk? Only those who wished to would buy our periodicals. People could read the article, "Don't be a corpse among the living!" in *Smena* and in *The Young Christian* they could read the answer to it. This is no more than justice and only in this way can one interpret freedom.

As for anti-religious propaganda, we do not fear it. Do you really think that your lies would attract a man who has recognized the truth, who has accepted Christ into his heart? People think very little, and this is one of the reasons for disbelief, but there is another reason – lack of will to accept the truth, because "it does not follow their fancies", nor does it "tickle their ears".

"For the time will come when they will not stand wholesome teaching; but shall follow their own fancy and gather a crowd of teachers to tickle their ears" (II Tim. 4:3).

Men who have not accepted the truth will "believe a lie" (2 Thess. 2:11). Only those who have not accepted the truth, who have not received Christ, will believe a lie. So for a Christian anti-religious propaganda is not dangerous.

You write: "We atheists are not against eternal life, but it must exist here, on earth, not in a world beyond. Immortality consists for us not, as religion promises, in sitting idly in some sort of Elysian field, munching sticky buns and unconcernedly watching the larger part of humanity suffer agony in fiery Gehenna."

I do not know what "religion promises", but the Word of God says this: "For the kingdom of God is not meat and drink; but righteousness, and peace, and joy in the Holy Ghost" (Rom. 14:17).

You write: "Man achieves immortality through his work."

Even the very fact that you talk about immortality shows that despite your atheism, you find it hard to conceive that you will disappear for ever. From your point of view, we can do no more than talk, firstly, about the immortality of great men such as Pushkin, Lomonosov, Beethoven and, if you wish, Gagarin; and, secondly, about that of men who create material things. Take for example militant atheists whose lives have been dedicated to fighting religion: what will they leave behind them? What works of genius?

Perhaps such brilliant lines as these:

Priest Naum knocked some
Sense into a peasant woman;
And so she sold a sucking-pig
And to the priest her gains did give

No doubt humanity, filled with gratitude, will immortalize the author's name.

In general it must be said that up to now very little glory has fallen to the lot of atheists. Over the last twenty centuries there have been a great many cruel persecutors and derogators of Christ's name, but for some reason people have forgotten their names, except for Herod, Caiaphas and Nero. Even those who persecute Christians today do not pronounce these names with respect.

Yes, there have been many derogators of Christ's name over the last twenty centuries but they have died and the world has forgotten their names, whilst before the name of Christ millions of people all over the world have bowed . . .

"Baptists see the meaning of life in getting themselves well-prepared for the after-life", you state.

Here is what Oswald Smith has to say on this subject: "You can work away at perfecting your character even until the day of judgment, but nevertheless you will meet with utter and complete defeat. Every birth is a crisis, and spiritual birth is no exception. New life is gained not by the growth, development or evolution of one's previous life but by means of a spiritual revolution. When Christ enters your heart you become his child, his property. If he has gained possession of you, then all the rest is no longer difficult. Christ creates his own image in you, he dwells in you, transforms you from within."

The goal of our life is "to build communism and live under it".

One feels like saying to you: "Is not the life more than meat, and the body than raiment?" (Matt. 6:25).

In your opinion, there is no nobler, brighter or more beautiful goal in the world than that of building communism and living under it. And you ask me whether I am prepared to work for this goal.

No, I do not want to work for this goal because I consider it neither bright nor noble. The society which you will build will never be just, because you yourselves are unjust. I am deeply convinced that where there is no truth, there can be no happiness either.

The goal of my life is to serve the truth.

My father refused to kill people. You call this a crime. He refused to kill people and for this he lost his own life. He died in order not to kill. If everyone were prepared to die rather than to kill, then there would be no wars. Christ said, "Do not kill". You jeer at this commandment. If only people would remember it! But today some have forgotten it, others jeer at it and that is the only reason why today the threat of war hangs over the world.

This is the only reason—there are no others!

Are we threatened with war because many other people refuse to take up arms?

"Your father," you say, "refused to take up arms to defend you." You say "defend". I know Baptists who did take up arms to defend their children, their homeland. But today in this county, in the country which they defended, they are rejected; they are not trusted, they are forbidden to meet freely for prayer, a whole stream of crude lies pours down upon them and they are told, "There is no room for you in our beautiful world!", "You're getting in our way!", "We'll isolate you!", "We'll punish you!".

What advice for defending their children would you give those Baptists today who took up arms to defend their children from the Fascists? You say that the question is not one of physical punishment for believers but of an ideological struggle. But why then are our best brothers in prison?

You say: "Innumerable are the crimes of all religions, including the Baptist faith, before humanity and particularly before science."

"All religions," you say.

We are not concerned with religions. There are many religions, some with difficult and complex rituals, some thought up by men. The Christian religion without the living Christ is powerless: such a religion does not save; it is dead and cannot enable a man to be born again. We are not religious people – we are Christians.

May we remind you that in so-called Christian Russia those who preached Christ's Gospel were thrown into prison and sent to Siberia. One would have thought that in a Christian country there would have been freedom to preach the Gospel. But they were arrested for preaching the Gospel and those who met to read it and pray were dispersed.

At the moment our country no longer calls itself Christian. It is an atheist country. In our day, too, men are imprisoned for preaching the Gospel, and also those who meet to read the Bible and pray are dispersed.

Formerly "Christians" banned the preaching of the Gospel – now it is atheists who ban it.

What is the difference between the one and the other? Perhaps it is only in name that they differ. Do not let such a comparison outrage you. Believe me, it is of no importance to us by what name our persecutors call themselves. You are very proud of your atheism, you discuss cybernetics and atomic energy but threaten all those who care to talk about Christ, exactly as though you were some little country priest of days gone by. You have taken the baton from those who masqueraded in cassocks and fiercely persecuted Christians.

Jan Hus was burnt by men who called themselves Christians. He said:

> "O, Lord Jesus Christ, I am ready to bear with joy a cruel and terrible death for the sake of your shining Gospel and for preaching your Holy Word. Forgive, I beseech thee, all my enemies. For the main goal of all my preaching, teaching, writing and other works has been to save men from sin. And now I am called before the Roman Curia to answer for preaching the Gospel."

Today you do not want to admit that Jan Hus was burnt as a preacher of the Gospel. And this is quite understandable. You, after all, are also persecuting men for preaching the Gospel. And if you were to admit that Jan Hus was executed for preaching it, you would by this very admission condemn yourselves.

If Jan Hus had lived in our time, in our country, he would have been thrown into prison.

"During the Inquisition more than five million people were burnt and tortured in prison," you write, and you look amongst the burnt and tortured for atheists; but atheists were among those who did the torturing and burning. And there were Christians who protested against the witch-hunts, murders, plunder and violence. God's true children boldly went forth into battle armed with a formidable weapon. Before this weapon the transgressors trembled. This weapon was the Word of God, the teaching of Christ.

"It now behoves true and fearless martyrs for Christ, armed with the Gospel and with sword in hand – which is the Word of God – to fight against the evil designs of the Anti-Christ," said Jan Hus.

Why is it that during almost two thousand years of its existence the Christian religion has not raised society's moral standards you ask, and then give the following advice: "Don't trouble yourselves; you've got no answer". And yet it is not at all difficult to give you an answer. Society's moral standards have not risen because, as Christ said, "Men loved darkness rather than light" (John 3:19). Only very few followed Christ. The majority did not accept the Christian religion. Religion without Christ is dead and, consequently, it cannot enable a man to be born again, nor can it destroy evil.

You are deeply convinced (or try to convince yourselves and others) that religion "cripples a man morally", that religion "teaches a man to lie and dissemble", that religion represents "social stagnation" – in a word, religion is an evil and it should be fought "with tenacity and persistence". To fight evil is, of course, an admirable desire, but one should not forget Christ's remarkable words in the Gospel:

> "And why beholdest thou the mote that is in thy brother's eye, but considerest not the beam that is in thine own eye? Or how wilt thou say to thy brother, let me pull out the mote out of thine eye; and, behold, a beam is in thine own eye? Thou hypocrite, first cast out the beam out of thine own eye; and then shalt thou see clearly to cast out the mote out of thy brother's eye" (Matt. 7:3-5).

Here is the last point to which I would like to draw your attention. You are shocked that God destroyed all men save Noah's family. The ark was built in 120 years; for 120 years men heard the words: "Come in!", "Receive salvation", "Repent!", "Repent!". At last the ark was ready – and even then its doors remained open for six days. Anyone who wished could go in. But people did not want to. They perished – and it was simply because they did not wish to be saved. You have many times already heard God's call: "Repent before it is too late! Repent and inherit eternal life! Come to Christ!"

Just as in the past men were offered the ark as a means of salvation, so we have been given Christ. But you do not wish to receive Christ, you do not wish to receive eternal life. God offers you this life, but you do not wish to receive it. God offers you this life, but you reject the opportunity. Whom will you blame on the Day of Judgment? Who will bear the guilt for your downfall? Will it not be you yourselves? You were offered salvation so many times, but you did not want to "enter the ark".

But today you can still change your fate. Before it is too late,

COME TO CHRIST!

September 1962.[2]

2. Russian text: *Possev*, Frankfurt, No. 9, 1968, pp. 59–62.

VI

THE TRIAL[1]

[*The trial was held on* 11, 12 *and* 15 *July* 1968 *in Leningrad. The names of those composing the court were: Malinina (Judge), Otto, Varlamova (People's Assessors) and Timofeeva (Procurator).*[2] *The Judge opened the trial with the question:*]

Defendant, do you accept the competence of the court to try your case?

Aida: Yes.

Judge: You have no objection to the composition of the court?

Aida: No, but I have a request to make to it.

Judge: What request?

Aida: I decline a defence counsel and I request to be allowed to conduct my own defence.[3]

Judge: What is your opinion, comrade Procurator?

Procurator: I consider that the accused cannot conduct her own defence. She has been in a psychiatric hospital. I consider that a defence counsel should be present.

Judge: What is your opinion, defendant?

Aida: I have never been declared mentally ill. There was an examination – the investigator requested it[4] – and the examina-

1. The transcript of Aida's trial reached the west written out on twenty sheets of cloth, cut down from sheets or some other such article. Here we reproduce it almost in full, except for summarized passages in italics, or short omissions, marked thus '. . .'

2. The Procuracy is responsible for ensuring the correct observance of legality and for prosecuting in most criminal cases. People's Assessors in theory fulfill functions similar to those of the jury in a Western Court, but in addition they can intervene in the proceedings.

3. It is common knowledge that only in the rarest cases will Soviet defence lawyers put a real case for their clients.

4. In the last few years an increasing number of people, arrested for dissident views, have been designated as mentally ill, although in most cases psychiatrists outside the USSR can find no evidence for such a diagnosis. In this way the so-called patient can be put straight into a mental hospital and not brought to trial.

tion gave the conclusion that mentally I was completely healthy. And I have never suffered from any mental illness whatsoever. The results of the examination are here in court, you can look at them. If you find it possible to put me on trial, then that means you must give me the chance to defend myself.

Judge: For what reasons do you refuse a defence counsel?

Perhaps you find it materially difficult to hire a lawyer?

Aida: No.

Judge: Perhaps you refuse a defence counsel because the participation of a lawyer in the case is against your religious convictions?

Aida: No.

Judge: Have you something personal against the lawyer Denisov, or do you refuse any defence counsel?

Aida: I have nothing personal against the lawyer Denisov, I refuse any defence.

Judge: Explain why you refuse a defence lawyer?

Aida: I am charged with distributing literature allegedly containing deliberately false statements slandering the Soviet state and social order. I know the content of this literature well, better than a lawyer could. I consider that because of the nature of the charge against me, I can conduct my own defence. I am categorically against a defence counsel in this case. I have never heard of a defence being forced on someone against his will.

Judge: What is your opinion, comrade lawyer?

Lawyer: The right to a defence is upheld by the Constitution and every defendant can make use of this right and hire a lawyer. But it is not obligatory, a defendant can conduct his own defence. From what Skripnikova has said, it follows that she is familiar with the content of the literature which she distributed herself. I ask that her request be granted.

Procurator: I consider that Skripnikova's refusal of a defence counsel is unfounded. She is not well-versed in law, and in addition her education does not make her able to conduct her own defence. The appointment of a defence counsel does not conflict with her religious convictions. I think that her request should be turned down.

Judge: The court has conferred and has decided that she be allowed to conduct her own defence.

(The defence lawyer leaves the courtroom.)

Judge: The witnesses Lyudmila Skripnikova, Zinaida Skripnikova, Yevseeva, Boiko and Zvereva have not appeared in court. What is your opinion, comrade Procurator, about this; do you think it is possible to begin the hearing in the absence of these witnesses?

Procurator: Yes, I do.

Judge: What is your opinion, defendant?

Aida: I do not object to the absence of the witnesses Yevseeva and Zvereva. But I would like the witnesses Yekaterina Boiko, Lyudmila Skripnikova and particularly Zinaida Skripnikova to be present.

Judge: The court will inquire and find out why these witnesses have not appeared for the trial.

Judge: The indictment reads:—

Indictment in case no. 12010 against Aida Milkhailovna Skripnikova on commission of a crime as covered by article 190/1 of the Criminal Code of the RSFSR. The investigation in the present case established the following: Skripnikova, being a member of an unregistered so-called Evangelical Christian and Baptist Community in Leningrad, belonging to the illegally operating Council of Churches of Evangelical Christians and Baptists (CCECB), during 1967-1968, living in Leningrad without a residence permit and being without regular work, systematically distributed among Soviet citizens and also among foreign subjects literature illegally published by the CCECB, such as the journals *Fraternal Leaflet* and *Herald of Salvation,* various reports and appeals, containing deliberately false statements slandering the Soviet state and social order.

Thus on 7 November 1967, in the flat of citizen Yevseeva at Flat 7, No. 21, Third Sovetsyaka Street, Skripnikova met the Swedish subject Miss Jursmar, who had come to Leningrad as a tourist, and handed over to her for distribution abroad the following illegal publications of the CCECB, containing deliberately false statements slandering the Soviet state and social order:— one copy of the journal *Herald of Salvation* No. 19, 11 copies of the journal *Fraternal Leaflet* Nos. 9, 10, 11 for 1965, Nos. 5, 6, 11, 12 for 1966, Nos. 2, 5, 6 (2 copies) for 1967, brochures with condensed transcripts of the trials of members of the unregistered co-called ECB community in Ryazan.

Jursmar tried to take the literature she had received out of the country, but at the customs inspection the above-mentioned literature was discovered and confiscated.

In January 1968 Skripnikova sent to her friend David in a foreign state a copy of the journal *Herald of Salvation* No. 20 containing deliberately false statements slandering the Soviet state and social order. In the winter of 1968 Skripnikova sent her sister Zinaida Skripnikova at Flat 38, 2A Bakhmeteva Street for distribution among members of the unregistered ECB community two copies of the journal *Fraternal Leaflet* containing deliberately false statements slandering the Soviet state and social order. The above mentioned journals were received by Zinaida Skripnikova and given to members of the community.

In the winter 1967-1968 Skripnikova several times by book post sent her friend Shishkina at Ogorodnikova village, Kiknursky District, Kirov Region, copies of the journal *Herald of Salvation* containing deliberately false statements slandering the Soviet state and social order. In particular, she sent Nos. 11, 15, 18, 19 and others.

When questioned as a defendant, Skripnikova did not admit her guilt, but explained that she had in fact given Jursmar and sent to David, her sister and citizen Shiskina various CCECB publications, so in fact Skripnikova does not deny that she distributed literature published by the CCECB. At the same time, she declared that she considered that these publications contained no deliberately false statements slandering the Soviet state and social order, but as she put it, these statements only ". . . accurately reflect the situation of the church in our country . . ." However her guilt in distributing works containing deliberately false statements slandering the Soviet state and social order is fully established by the following evidence:

1. From the text of the literature given by Skripnikova to Jursmar and confiscated from the latter, from the text of *Herald of Salvation* No. 20 sent by Skripnikova to David (an identical copy was confiscated during a search at Skripnikova's home) and of others sent by Skripnikova to citizen Shishkina

(identical copies were confiscated during the search) from the text of the journals *Fraternal Leaflet* sent by Skripnikova to her sister (identical copies were confiscated from Skripnikova during the search) it follows that in all these publications there are deliberately false statements slandering the Soviet state and social order.

2. The fact that it was Skripnikova who gave the literature to Jursmar and sent it to David, Shiskina and Zinaida Skripnikova is established by the following evidence:

(a) the testimony of the witness Skurlova who declared that she had brought Jursmar to meet Skripnikova,

(b) the report on the confiscation of literature from Jursmar, given her by Skripnikova,

(c) the testimony of the witness Zinaida Skripnikova who explained that she had received from Aida Skripnikova literature published by the CCECB,

(d) the letter of Aida Skripnikova of 15 January 1968 in which she mentions sending David the journal *Herald of Salvation,*

(e) the letter of Shiskina at Skripnikova's, from which it is evident that Skripnikova sent literature published by the CCECB to Shishkina,

(f) the testimony of Skripnikova herself.

Besides this the guilt of Skripnikova in the systematic distribution of literature published by the CCECB and containing deliberately false statements slandering the Soviet state and social order is confirmed also by the fact that at the search of Skripnikova's room a quantity of literature was confiscated, illegally published by the CCECB, including individual publications in several copies. In particular, the following were confiscated from her: 25 copies of the journal *Fraternal Leaflet,* including 2 copies of No. 10, 1966, 2 copies of No. 9-10, 1967; 13 copies of the journal *Herald of Salvation* were confiscated, including 3 copies of the No. 11, 2 copies of No. 19 (a third copy was given to Jursmar), 2 copies of No. 20 (and a third was sent to David).

Besides this, the following brochures were confiscated from her during the search: a transcript of the trial of Kryuchkov and Vins[5] (one copy of this was given to Jursmar), a trans-

5. See M. Bourdeaux, *Faith on Trial in Russia,* London 1971, Chap. V.

cript of the trial of Golev and others (a copy was given to Jursmar), a transcript of the trial of Bondar and others in Alma-Ata, a transcript of the trial of Klassen and others in Dzhambul, a transcript of the trial of Makhovitsky in two copies.

In addition, a large quantity of other literature illegally published by the CCECB was also confiscated from her.

The very fact that such a large quantity of literature was confiscated testifies that Skripnikova has for some time been systematically distributing this literature.

Judge: Defendant, do you understand the charge against you?

Aida: Yes.

Judge: Do you plead guilty?

Aida: No.

Judge: The court has conferred and has decided to commence the hearing with the cross-examination of the defendant.

Cross-examination

Judge: Defendant, do you wish to give the court an explanation concerning the charge against you?

Aida: Yes, I do. I admit the facts about distributing literature as mentioned in the indictment, and about the recipients as mentioned.

Judge: Name them.

Aida: I gave Miss Jursmar from Sweden a copy of the *Herald of Salvation* No. 19, several *Fraternal Leaflets*, transcripts of trials in Moscow and Ryazan; to my sister in Magnitogorsk I sent a copy of *Herald of Salvation*; to Shishkina at Ogorodnika village, Kirov region, I sent copies of *Herald of Salvation* Nos. 11, 15, 18, 19. I may have sent her some other numbers. I don't remember. And I sent a copy of *Herald of Salvation* to David abroad.

Judge: To where exactly did you send David *Herald of Salvation* No. 20, to what country?

Aida: I sent it to Sweden. I'd like to make one remark about the indictment. In the indictment *Fraternal Leaflet* is called a journal. It's not a journal, it's a leaflet, usually two or three pages. There are copies of it among the evidence, which were taken from me during the search. I sent my sister in Magnitogorsk a copy of *Herald of Salvation*, not *Fraternal Leaflets.*

Judge: Everything else in the indictment is correct?

Aida: Yes. All the facts about the distribution of literature are correct. But this literature does not contain deliberately false statements slandering the Soviet state and social order, that is, this does not constitute a crime under article 190/1, and the distribution of literature in itself is not a crime, therefore I plead not guilty.

Judge: Where and when did you get to know Jursmar?

Aida: I won't answer that question, because that's a private matter.

Judge: We're not asking you this question because we want to interfere in your private life. You're charged with giving Jursmar literature, therefore the court is interested in your friendship with her.

Aida: All right, I'll tell you. I have a good Christian friend in Sweden, Bengt Persson. And when Jursmar came to Leningrad, Bengt gave her my address so that she could visit me. If I go to some other town, for example to Perm, then the believers in Leningrad can give me the address of their friends in Perm so that I can visit them. That's how it was in this case.

Judge: Before Jursmar came to see you, you didn't know her?

Aida: No.

Judge: Did Jursmar tell you where she works, what she does?

Aida: She told me she works as a typist.

Judge: Where does she work as a typist, do you know?

Aida: She works at the Slavic Mission.

Judge: Indeed, the Slavic Mission.

Aida: Well? So what? The Slavic Mission is a religious organization, and no jurist in the world can ever call it anything else.

Judge: What did Jursmar bring you?

Aida: New Testaments.

Judge: How many?

Aida: Fifty. But the police took them from me.

Judge: Who did these New Testaments come from?

Aida: It's all the same to me.

Judge: What were you going to do with such a large number of New Testaments?

Aida: Give them out.

Judge: To whom?

Aida: To believers who do not have one.

Procurator: The New Testaments that Jursmar brought you, what was their content?
Aida: They were the same as any New Testament.
Procurator: The content of a New Testament depends on the edition. It depends on where it was published.
Aida: The content of a New Testament is never altered. They're always the same. If we had enough New Testaments, I wouldn't be getting them from abroad. It's all the same to me where they're printed, in Moscow or in Stockholm.
Judge: Why did you give Jursmar copies of the *Herald of Salvation* and *Fraternal Leaflet*, transcripts of trials in Moscow and Ryazan, and letters of Khorev and Makhovitsky?
Aida: So that she could read them and find out about the life of our church. The journal *Herald of Salvation* is my favourite journal. The *Fraternal Leaflets* speak about the life of our church. Trials have become so much a part of our church life that to know about the Russian church, you must know about the trials.
Judge: Was this literature intended only for Jursmar?
Aida: No, for other believers too.
Judge: You were completely unacquainted with Jursmar until 7 November. And then you give a foreign subject, a Swedish citizen, whom you hardly know, the journal *Herald of Salvation* and private letters. Were you sure that this unknown foreigner would not use the literature received from you for harmful purposes?
Aida: With believers, friendships develop more simply. I can go to a strange town, meet believers, whom I didn't know before, and after a few minutes we can become close friends.
Judge: You gave Jursmar copies of *Fraternal Leaflet*, and transcripts of trials so that, as you put it, they could get to know about the life of your church there; but then why did you give her letters by Khorev and Makhovitsky?
Aida: They're interesting letters.
Judge: The letters of Khorev and Makhovitsky don't contain deliberately false statements. You're not charged with passing them on. But why did you give them? After all, they're private letters. Makhovitsky is writing to his wife and children. Who could be interested in this letter?
Aida: Believers are one big family and we are interested in everything about each other.

Judge: Makhovitsky's letter in itself does not contain deliberately false statements, but when it is put with all the literature saying that in this country people are persecuted for their faith, then there must be a particular reason for sending it: to show Makhovitsky, the father of seven children, sentenced for his faith, is suffering in prison and longing for his children. Makhovitsky certainly was sentenced, but not for his faith – for illegal activity.
Procurator: Did Makhovitsky ask you to pass on his letter?
Aida: No.
Procurator: How could you pass on a private letter without permission?
Judge: There is a law protecting the secrecy of private correspondence.
Procurator: You are breaking that law.
Aida: If Makhovitsky's wife brings a court case against me for violating the secrecy of her correspondence, well then I'll have to answer before this law!
Procurator: (laughing) Of course she won't bring a court case against you.
Judge: When you gave the literature to Jursmar, did you consider how she might use it?
Aida: No, I didn't. She could dispose of it as she thought best.
Judge: But you didn't think of the fact that the literature could be used against our country?
Aida: Jursmar is a believer like me. I trust her. The literature that I gave her is good. It could not in any way be used for harmful ends.
Procurator: The evidence includes a notebook confiscated from you during the search. Does it belong to you?
Aida: Yes.
Procurator: In your notebook there are a lot of foreign addresses: did you have correspondence with all of them?
Aida: With some of them. I don't know any law forbidding one to correspond with friends abroad.

[*There follows a list of names, with whom Aida was in contact.*]

Procurator: What time did Jursmar come to you?
Aida: She came at about half past eight in the evening.
Procurator: Did you talk together?

Aida: Yes.

Procurator: What did you talk about?

Aida: We told each other about ourselves and about the church.

Procurator: A notebook was confiscated from Jursmar; did she make notes from what you said?

Aida: I saw Jursmar's notebook and a translation of it among the evidence, but I don't understand all the notes.

Procurator: Jursmar's notebook is a short account of what happened that evening. A sort of consultation between Jursmar and Skripnikova. What questions did they discuss? A whole programme of action was worked out. Stirring up foreign bodies to address letters and protests to members of the Soviet government. Organize a series of broadcasts on the B.B.C. and Voice of America. Tell us, defendant, what questions did you discuss with Jursmar?

Aida: I don't remember all our conversation. There's nothing in the notebook about a series of broadcasts on the B.B.C. She only wrote B.B.C. – that's all.

Judge: In Jursmar's notebook there's this note: "Three awaiting trial in Leningrad: a man and two women." That's obviously about Zhukova, Lukas and Semenova. They were under investigation at that time. Did you tell Jursmar about that?

Aida: I don't remember. I may have told her that three people had been arrested in Leningrad. I can't remember everything we talked about.

Judge: If three of your fellow believers had been arrested, surely you would have told her about that. It must have been worrying you at the time. It's hard to believe that in talking to Jursmar you wouldn't have mentioned it.

Aida: It looks as if I did tell her, of course I must have done.

Judge: Jursmar has written: "One of the women is expecting a child." Who is meant here?

Aida: I don't know why that's written there, it's difficult to understand somebody else's notes. Neither Zhukova nor Semenova has any children, Lukas has six children.

Judge: Jursmar has written a note about the amnesty,[6] claiming that it didn't apply to believers. Did she write that down from what you said?

6. This refers to the amnesty declared in 1967 on the occasion of the 50th anniversary of the October revolution.

Aida: I don't know, maybe I told her about the amnesty, I don't remember.

Procurator: But Jursmar didn't meet anybody else except you.

Aida: I don't remember talking to Jursmar about the amnesty. She wrote, "Believers are considered dangerous criminals". She could have written that as her own conclusion, because believers have not been released under the amnesty. Of course I could have told Jursmar that the amnesty did not apply to believers. I simply can't remember all that we talked about. We probably did talk about the amnesty. Everybody was waiting for it, both we and our brothers and sisters abroad, but it hardly benefitted believers.

Judge: The decree about the amnesty was issued on 31 October. You met Jursmar on 7 November. You realize that by that time no one could have been amnestied. The liberation committees were just beginning to function, but you were already telling people abroad that the amnesty didn't apply to believers.

Aida: My friends had written to me from prison-camp and said that they had been called before the commission and that they hadn't been freed.

Judge: You're getting confused. They couldn't have written you that by 7 November.

Procurator: The amnesty was applied at the trials of Lukas, Zhukova and Semenova. The court sentenced them to three years, but the decree on the amnesty was applied and cut it by 1½ years. But you were telling people abroad that the amnesty didn't affect believers.

Aida: I wrote to Persson later and told him that the amnesty had been applied to Lukas, Zhukova and Semenova and 1½ years taken off. But in general they applied the amnesty to hardly any believers.

Judge: You were well acquainted with the contents of the literature you gave to Jursmar?

Aida: Yes.

Judge: Do you consider that the real situation is truly represented in the literature you passed on?

Aida: Yes.

Judge: You gave Jursmar a transcript of the trial in Ryazan. Are you sure that this transcript is accurate, that what was written down is what was said at the trial? From here, you see, I can clearly note what is happening in the courtroom. Some people started to try and take it all down. But what can you note down in such conditions? A few words. Would this be a transcript of the trial?[7]

Aida: I was at the trial in Ryazan and there the conditions for a transcript were better. It was done quite well and the speech of the Procurator was very well transcribed.

Judge: The journal *Herald of Salvation* No. 19 speaks of persecution. In the article "A century's path of struggle and suffering"[8] it says that believers are victimized, dismissed from work and excluded from educational institutions, but specific facts are not cited. It doesn't state who's been dismissed from work and expelled from educational institutions, nor where, nor when.

Aida: The article was written in general terms.

Judge: There must be facts. You can write what you will, but facts must be supported. You must have thought about that when you sent the journal abroad.

Aida: To have cited the facts in the *Herald of Salvation* would have been out of place: the articles would then have turned out very long. When the Council of Prisoners' Relatives[9] wrote to the General Secretary of the United Nations, U Thant, specific facts about persecutions were pointed out in the letter.

Procurator: In the article "A century's path of struggle and suffering" it says that there's persecution of believers in the Soviet Union, people are dismissed from work and not allowed to study: but not one fact is cited. You send this journal abroad and there they will draw their own conclusions; that in general all believers in the Soviet Union are persecuted.[10] You don't cite specific facts.

Aida: The *Herald of Salvation* isn't published for people

7. Several detailed accounts of trials such as Aida's have been made, despite the difficult conditions.

8. This article was written by Aida and others at the time of the centenary (1967) commemorating the founding of the Baptist church in Russia.

9. This organization, set up by a group of Baptist women, collects all information on ECB prisoners and periodically draws up lists containing each prisoner's name and other details.

10. For information on the recent difficulties and suffering undergone

abroad. All we believers know very well about persecution. The history of the church is described in the article "A century's path of struggle and suffering" and it's a true description. But the facts can't be enumerated, otherwise one article, such as this one, would take up the whole journal.

Procurator: Do you recognize other denominations?

Aida: What do you mean?

Procurator: In the Soviet Union there are various denominations. Do you recognize them?

Aida: I recognize them, I don't share their convictions, but I do recognize that they exist.

Procurator: You write about the persecution of believers, but do you know about persecution of believers of other denominations?

Aida: I don't know about the persecution of believers of other denominations, we write only about the persecution of believers of the Evangelical Christian and Baptist Church.

Procurator: You write and don't point out the facts, but abroad surely, they could think that all believers in general are persecuted in this country?

Aida: I don't know.

Judge: You know there will be people who will read this in all sorts of ways. At the trial[11] in Moscow, Vins said that there are believers there who are persecuted and again he does not cite the facts.

Aida: Vins did cite facts.

Judge: Vins simply said that believers were being dismissed from their jobs. But he doesn't cite the facts.

Aida: Kryuchkov gave several names of believers who were taken straight from work and tried in accordance with the decree on parasites.[12]

by the Russian Orthodox Church, see Michael Bourdeaux *Patriarch and Prophets*, London, 1969, chapters 2, 3, and 4. On the persecution of the Uniate Church in Lithuania, see for example *A Chronicle of Current Events*, Amnesty International Publications, No. 21, pp. 287–288 and No. 23, pp. 79–84.

11. The trial of Kryuchkov and Vins (leaders of the reform movement) was held on 29–30 November, 1966. See Michael Bourdeaux *Faith on Trial*, London, 1971, pp. 110–130.

12. The Decree on the campaign against parasitism was introduced by Khrushchev in 1961.

Procurator: Kryuchkov said that prayer houses were being demolished by bulldozers.[13] With urban re-planning houses are sometimes demolished by bulldozers and among those are prayer houses. But this does *not* mean that believers are oppressed. In Leningrad in the Okhta district a prayer house was demolished.

Aida: In Leningrad a prayer house was demolished in the Okhta district, but a prayer house was given to a registered community on Poklonnaya Hill and no one said and no one wrote that they had taken away a prayer house. In Vladivostok for example, a prayer house was demolished by a bulldozer and they didn't give them a replacement. When prayer houses are destroyed and they give you no replacement then our people say that believers have been deprived of a prayer house. Kryuchkov did speak about this at his trial. He named towns where they took away prayer houses.

Procurator: In Leningrad when the prayer house was demolished in the Okhta district they also said that believers were being deprived of a prayer house and went and complained.

Aida: I never heard anything about this.

Procurator: In the *Herald of Salvation* No. 15 it is said that believers' children are persecuted in school.[14] What's this persecution, what kind of persecution do these children undergo?

Aida: Children are taken away from their parents because of their Christian upbringing. Two such cases are described in the letter to U Thant. In Kazan a daughter was taken away from believers; the two children of the Christian Sloboda family[15] in the Vitebsk region were taken away from them. In Smolensk the son of Lidia Govorun was taken away; it's true that he was then returned after a time. I can't state other

13. See also Appeal II in R. Harris and X. Howard-Johnston *Christian Appeals from Russia*, London, 1969, p. 42, where two private houses, one in Barnaul and the other Vladivostok, were demolished by bulldozer because prayer meetings were held there.

14. On the interrogation of children in school see *Christian Appeals from Russia*, pp. 46–47.

15. See the appeal written by Mr. and Mrs. Sloboda in *Christian Appeals from Russia*, pp. 87–89. The three younger children have also now been put in a state home and their mother imprisoned, according to a letter written by Mr. Sloboda in March 1970.

facts now, I simply don't remember names, but there were other cases as well when believers' children were taken away from them.

Procurator: You keep telling us about other towns, but let's talk about Leningrad. Have they taken away children from anying in Leningrad?

Aida: No, there have been no such cases in Leningrad.

Procurator: But is there persecution of children in schools? What sort of persecution is it?

Aida: They question children in schools.

Procurator: Who questions them?

Aida: The men from the procurator's office. They take a child from a lesson and question him for several hours. Parents have reported this.

Procurator: By law men from the procurator's office can question those under age if it's essential for a case. Both believers' and unbelievers' children can be questioned. When they started the criminal case against Zhukova it was essential to question several children, because she was accused of organizing religious activities with children. Questioning of those under age does not contravene the law. This isn't persecution.

Aida: But they asked children about belief. Sometimes children are kept behind after lessons; they chat with them; they say that they mustn't go to the meetings; they mustn't listen to their parents when they talk about God.

Procurator: Provision is made by law for anti-religious education in schools.

Aida: If a teacher at a lesson carries on an anti-religious conversation with all the children, all right; but when they leave a child alone after lessons and carry on a conversation with him separately, it's a different matter. An adult can deal calmly with such conversations, but for a child this can cause a trauma. Children have lived under the fear that they would be taken to a state home.[16] I could name such children in Leningrad, but I do not want to cause anxiety to these families.

Procurator: The law forbids the imposition of belief on those under age.

Aida: But the law does not forbid the imposition of atheism.

16. This happened to all five children of the Sloboda family.

Procurator: Atheism isn't religion. A child grows up and then he must himself decide his attitude towards belief. Atheism isn't imposed.
Aida: Then what does one say to a child? That one is forbidden, by law, to say that God exists, but to say that there is no God is allowed?
Judge: Will the defendant not digress from the main point.
Procurator: The *Fraternal Leaflet* Nos. 5-6 for 1965 states, "We shall pray that it should conform to the highest principles of goodness, peace and justice." Here the Constitution is the subject. The government had proposed to work out a project for a new constitution, and here in the *Fraternal Leaflet* they write: "We shall pray that the new constitution should conform to the highest principles of goodness, peace and justice." Abroad they could conclude that the Constitution at present in force does not conform to these principles.
Aida: You can understand it in two ways.
Procurator: That's exactly the point – all your literature can be understood in two ways. What laws relating to religion do you know?
Aida: I know the Constitution, I know article 124 of it and the decree of 1929; I know the law on the separation of the church from the state.[17]
Procurator: You know that a religious community must be registered?[18]
Aida: Yes.
Procurator: Your community did not register, therefore you are prevented from holding meetings, but not because there's persecution of believers in our country.
Aida: Our community requested registration. We put in an application but we were refused.
Procurator: You were refused because you refuse to observe the law.
Aida: Which laws do we not observe?

17. Article 124 in the Constitution guarantees Soviet citizens freedom of conscience. The 1929 *Laws on Religious Associations*, referred to here as "the decree of 1929", were introduced by Stalin to restrict the church's activity. The law on the separation of church and state and of schools from the church was adopted in 1918.
18. On registration see Chapter II *The Background*, p. 8.

Procurator: You're demanding the creation of Sunday schools and organize religious activities for children under age.
Aida: I don't remember that our comunity demanded a Sunday school. By law parents can bring up their children as they wish.
Procurator: No, they can't. It's forbidden by law to involve children under age in religious societies. But you refuse to reckon with our laws.
Aida: We aren't asking for anything which is illegal. I cannot understand what it is we are doing which is illegal.
Judge: Haven't you understood yet?
Aida: No, I haven't. According to the Constitution we have freedom of religious belief. The word implies a confession of faith. It means that it is possible to tell everyone about God – that is, to profess one's belief freely. We don't say of course that we'll stand up in the middle of the shop floor at work, during working hours and begin to preach. No one does *that*.
Judge: In a letter of 12 November 1967 addressed to Bengt, you write, "I was afraid that Lota would be tried for everything she took from us." You say that there are no deliberately false statements in the literature you passed on. In that case, why were you afraid she might be tried because of them?
Aida: Because persecutors don't like it when the fact of their persecution becomes known. I know that in the literature I gave Miss Jursmar there were no deliberately false statements. In the *Herald of Salvation* No. 19 and in the *Fraternal Leaflets* where the situation of believers is described, it's described as it really is. I agree with you that it's unattractive, but this *is* real life and it must be talked about. When I was handing over the literature to Miss Jursmar I knew that these persecutors could get me locked up. I understand that.
Procurator: In sending information abroad making out that in the Soviet Union believers are persecuted for their faith, and in handing over transcripts of trials, did you consider the fact that you would thus harm your country?
Aida: I knew that this wouldn't harm Russia. To bring disgrace on our persecutors is another matter; but shouldn't they perhaps be put to shame? Our country could be the most beautiful country in the world, were there no persecution here. Persecution only does harm. If there were no persecution, Russia would gain a great deal.

Procurator: We've got used to calling our country the Soviet Union. This denotes the state structure and is used also in the political sense. "Russia" is a geographical concept. What meaning do you attach to the word "Russia"?

Aida: I call our country "Russia", because this name is very dear to me. I include in the word "Russia" not only the geographical concept, but also the people and the customs which I love. As for the political meaning, I understand little about that.

Procurator: Whom do you mean by the word "persecutors"?

Aida: The atheists who've been given extensive rights to persecute believers.

Procurator: But why do they only persecute you, why don't they persecute other denominations?

Aida: I don't know about other denominations.

Procurator: But they'll come to the conclusion abroad that all believers are persecuted in the Soviet Union.

Aida: I don't know what conclusions people will come to there.

Procurator: Do you read any other literature besides religious literature?

Aida: I read fiction.

Procurator: And do you read the newspapers?

Aida: I look through them.

Procurator: Do you read any newspapers other than the *Herald of Salvation*?

Aida: Sometimes.

Procurator: Exactly which newspapers?

Aida: I don't know what to say . . . those which come my way.

Procurator: And do you go to the cinema?

Aida: No.

Procurator: Do you watch television?

Aida: No.

Procurator: How do you find out about the life of the Soviet people? You don't watch television, you don't go to the cinema, you don't read Soviet fiction.

Aida: The life of the people is in front of my eyes.

Procurator: But you haven't worked for a year in a workers' collective; you haven't had contact with them. Where could you see the life of the people? You stayed at home. Boiko used to come and see you and Skurlova and that was all.

Aida: I didn't stay at home all the time.

Procurator: I don't mean you didn't go out of the house. But all this time you went around in your own milieu. You couldn't know about the life of the people, and here you are introducing yourself to foreigners as a representative of the Russian church, and you yourself don't even know about the life of the people. How did you take on such a role?

Aida: I didn't introduce myself to foreigners as a representative of the Russian church. I'm an ordinary member of the community.

Procurator: I am not saying that you had any official authority. But foreigners saw you as a representative of the Russian church. How could you tell foreigners about the life of our people if you didn't know about it yourself?

Aida: I spoke only about what I know well. I told them about the life of believers.

Procurator: But you don't even know about the life of believers. You say that you're persecuted. But in our country there are other denominations; they aren't persecuted! Why is it just you who are persecuted?

Aida: I'm firmly convinced that a man who sincerely believes faithfully follows God and acts independently of what he is called whether he's Baptist or Orthodox. But we write only about our church because we know it well.

The Interrogation of the Witnesses

[*The witness Anatoli Lavrentev, a neighbour of Aida's from the communal flat where she lived, comes in and is warned under articles* 181 *and* 182 *about the responsibility of giving false evidence.*

The judge begins the interrogation with the question:]

Do you know the defendant?

Witness: Yes.

Judge: What sort of relationship do you have with her?

Witness: A good relationship.

Judge: Have you known the defendant long?

Witness: About a year.

Judge: How did you get to know her?

Witness: Our neighbour Evseyeva left and Aida remained living in her room.

Judge: What can you tell us about Aida?
Witness: Aida is a sensitive and sympathetic person.
Judge: What was Skripnikova's relationship with the other neighbours?
Witness: Skripnikova was on good terms with everyone. You could only speak good of her.
Judge: Were you interested in how Skripnikova managed to live?
Witness: We thought that she worked. She went out each morning.
Judge: Did Aida tell you where she worked?
Witness: Aida said she was employed in a printing works.
Judge: Who called on Skripnikova?
Witness: Maria – I don't know her surname – used to call on Skripnikova.
Judge: Did Aida tell you that she was a believer?
Witness: Aida didn't tell me, but I knew; I heard it from others.
Judge: Did you talk about this with her?
Witness: No. We had no conversations on this subject.
Judge: Did Aida give you any sort of literature?
Witness: No, Aida gave me no kind of literature.
Judge: (To the defendant) Was this, on your part, to ensure that attention was not drawn to you in the place where you lived?
Aida: No. Perhaps this was my mistake. We sometimes talked with the neighbours about faith, but they showed no interest and therefore I didn't offer them anything to read.
Procurator: How long did Skripnikova live in Evseyeva's room?
Witness: About a year.
Procurator: Did Evseyeva have a television?
Witness: No.
Procurator: A radio?
Witness: Yes, there was a radio.
Procurator: What programmes did Aida listen to?
Witness: I don't know. I didn't go into the room.
Procurator: But surely you could hear in the corridor?
Witness: I could hear that the radio was switched on, but I couldn't hear what was being said.
Procurator: What do you think: did Aida live according to

her means, or did you notice that she was not living according to her means?
Witness: No, Aida lived modestly.
Procurator: How did this show?
Witness: In her dress, and in her food.
Judge: What did Aida eat?
Witness: Simple things.
Judge: Did she buy herself anything in the way of clothes?
Witness: No, I didn't see anything.
Judge: But perhaps at some point she showed off to the neighbours, like women do, that she had bought a new dress, or something else?
Witness: No. That never happened.
Judge: Did you see any foreigners at Skripnikova's?
Witness: No.
Judge: (to the defendant) Do you have any questions to ask the witness?
Aida: Yes. Tell me please, when did I come to live in Evseyeva's room?
Witness: Around June 1967.
Aida: Can you perhaps remember more exactly?
Witness: Perhaps it was earlier, in May or even April.
Aida: I began living in this room on 9 April 1967.
Witness: Yes, that's right.
Aida: Did I tell you that I was employed in a printing works?
Witness: Yes, I remember that you told us that.
Aida: (to the Judge) When I came to live in Evseyeva's room I was still working there and said so to the neighbours. I was sacked on 21 April.

[*The witness Alla Lavrenteva, a neighbour from the flat where Aida lived, is now questioned by the Judge.*]

Judge: Do you know the defendant?
Witness: I know her.
Judge: How do you get on with her?
Witness: Very well.
Judge: How did you get to know Skripnikova?
Witness: About a year ago my neighbour Evseyeva was leaving and she said that a young girl would be living in her room.
Judge: What sort of impression did Aida make on you?

Witness: She seemed to me to be a nice girl; I saw Aida only in the kitchen.
Judge: Who used to call on Aida?
Witness: Aida's friend Maria used to.
Judge: Did you know that Aida was a believer?
Witness: Yes, I knew.
Judge: Did you have any conversations with her on this subject?
Witness: Yes.
Judge: Did you try to dissuade Aida?
Witness: Yes, I told her she ought not to believe.
Judge: Did you produce any arguments?
Witness: Yes, I told her that only the old believe in God.
Judge: But you had no serious conversations on this subject?
Witness: No, there were no serious conversations.
Judge: Did she offer you any sort of literature?
Witness: No.
Judge: How did Aida behave in the flat?
Witness: Very well.
Judge: She didn't quarrel with anyone?
Witness: No, in general we don't quarrel in the flat. We all get on well together.
Judge: A fortunate flat. How did Aida manage as regards money? How did she dress?
Witness: Modestly.
Judge: How did she eat?
Witness: Like us all.
Judge: What did she prepare in the kitchen?
Witness: Well, I'm not sure what to say. She cooked soup, cabbage soup, potatoes. Nothing special.
Judge: Were you interested in where Aida worked?
Witness: Aida said it was at the printing works. She used to leave in the morning.

[*The third witness to be questioned is called Emanuil Moiseyevich, also a neighbour of Aida from the flat where she lived.*]

Judge: Do you know the defendant?
Witness: Yes, I know her.
Judge: How do you know her?
Witness: Aida lived in our flat.
Judge: What did Skripnikova do?

Witness: I don't know. I leave for work in the morning and come back late in the evening. I saw Aida only in the evening.

Judge: What impression did Aida make on you?

Witness: Outwardly she made a very good impression .She is quiet, polite and modest.

Judge: Did Aida give any occasion for a quarrel in the flat?

Witness: No.

Judge: That means she was ideal as a neighbour.

Witness: Yes.

Judge: What did Aida eat, what did she cook?

Witness: I never used to interfere in these kitchen matters, you know; I rarely go into the kitchen.

Judge: Did you know what means Skripnikova had to live on?

Witness: We thought she worked.

Judge: Did Skripnikova tell you where she worked?

Witness: I heard it was at the printing works, but then she left there. I heard she was looking for work. I once had a chat with Aida about it. I work at the musical instrument factory in charge of production. Aida asked me whether it was possible for her to get a job at our place. I don't remember exactly whether Aida asked me or whether I myself suggested she get a job at our place. Then we somehow stopped talking about it and Aida said that she'd found a job.

[*Marfa Akimovna Skurlova now enters for questioning. She is a believer and close friend of Aida.*]

Judge: Do you know the defendant?

Witness: I know her very well.

Judge: Have you known her long?

Witness: About five years.

Judge: How did you come to know the accused?

Witness: We got to know each other at the prayer house.

Judge: How did you get on with Skripnikova?

Witness: Very well. Aida stayed with me.

Judge: Tell us, what did Aida do when she was staying with you?

Witness: I knew that Aida had lost her job and her residence permit, and invited her to come and stay with me. Aida was looking for work, she walked and travelled about everywhere. She got a job at Sestroretsk. She worked there for three months and they promised to provide her with a residence permit, but then they refused, so we found an old woman who wanted to register Aida at her place. This old woman was ill and lived alone. She wanted Aida to live with her and help her. Aida wanted to register at her home and get a job, but the police again refused. Then they arrested Aida. We had a meeting in the woods, the police arrived and began chasing us off. They pushed and grabbed us by the hair. They took away several people: some they fined and some they imprisoned for a fortnight. Aida was arrested and brought to trial. They said that she was being tried for not having a residence permit. And what a trial they organized. It wasn't a good court. She was brought to some factory; they shouted and made a noise; Aida wasn't even given a chance to speak. When Aida left prison she came to Leningrad. She registered in Volkhovstroye and got a job, but when they found out that she was a believer she was dismissed. Then we found out that Aida had been taken off the register of inhabitants and the police were looking for her.

Judge: Skripnikova was without work for almost a year. On what money did she live?

Witness: Skripnikova worked all the time. If she didn't have enough money she went out and worked.

Judge: Where did she work?

Witness: Let her tell you herself where she worked.

Judge: Did you help Skripnikova materially?

Witness: I have my own kitchen garden and sometimes I gave Aida vegetables.

Judge: You say that Aida was dismissed from her job because she was a believer. Why aren't you dismissed from your job; why is Boiko not dismissed? Surely you work.

Witness: My turn hasn't come yet.

Judge: Surely you don't think they would dismiss you from your work in dog breeding.

Witness: But you don't know how much people talk to me.

Judged: Did you have foreigners in on 7 November?

Witness: Yes.

Judge: Why did they call on you?

Witness: They wrote letters to Aida before and came along to our address.

Judge: They came to you, but what then?

Witness: They called and nothing more.
Judge: So they called and said nothing?
Witness: No, they spoke and said hello.
Judge: They said hello and that was all? "Hello, look we've come"?
Witness: No, they asked for Aida.
Judge: What did you say to them?
Witness: I said that Aida didn't live here. They asked to be taken to Aida and we set off there.
Judge: Did you phone Aida beforehand? Did you ask for permission to call?
Witness: Why should I ask her permission? I asked if she was at home and told her not to go out anywhere because we would arrive soon. Aida said "All right, I'll wait for you."
Judge: What did the foreigners bring?
Witness: They brought 50 New Testaments. We don't have enough Bibles and New Testaments.
Judge: So you were brought 50 copies.
Witness: And these were taken away.
Judge: Were you present when Skripnikova talked to the foreigners?
Witness: No, I wasn't. I went off home immediately.
Judge: Did you know that Aida gave them some literature?
Did she tell you about it?
Witness: No, Aida told me nothing. But what kind of literature could we have given them? We've got none.
Judge: And what about the literature lying on the table?
Witness: Surely that's not literature?
Judge: Oh! Has the defendant any questions to ask the witness?
Aida: Yes. After I was dismissed from the printing works what did I do?
Witness: After you were dismissed from the printing works you looked for a job.
Judge: Witness, you are to reply to the court. The defendant will ask you questions, but look this way as you reply to the court. Let the defendant continue.
Aida: Tell me, please, when did it become known that I had lost my residence permit?
Witness: I think it was in June.

Aida: When did they write to me about this from Volkhovstroye?
Witness: In September.
Aida: What happened in May 1967?
Witness: In May 1967 . . .
Aida: I mean what was it like in Leningrad in May 1967? Did our meetings go off peacefully or not? And what else happened in our church?
Witness: In May 1967, believers were not allowed to meet, they were harassed. There were searches at Lukas's place, and Protsenko's. I don't remember the names of the others who were searched. Believers were summoned to the Procurator's offices as witnesses. Then they arrested Semenova, Lukas and Zhukova.
Aida: In the Procurator's office did they ask questions about me?
Judge: Defendant, you are not to ask questions in that form. You are suggesting the answer in that way. Formulate your questions in a different way.
Aida: Very well, I will try. I want to clear up one question with the witnesses. The witness is confused; she says that I lost my residence permit and then the police began taking an interest in me. But it was the other way round. The Procurator's office began showing a lot of interest in May, and then I was crossed off the register.
Witness: Yes, I remember it well. They were asking about Aida in the Procurator's office in May when believers were being called in for questioning.
Judge: Defendant, do you have any questions for the witness?
Aida: Yes. What do you know about the fines? Can you name the believers who were fined?
Witness: I know that believers were fined: Sukovitsin was fined . . .
Procurator: Why was he fined?
Witness: Because he had prayed.
Procurator: Where had he prayed?
Witness: He led the prayers at Lukas's flat. There was a meeting there.
Procurator: That's right, a meeting in an unauthorized place. You have a prayer house, go and pray there.
Witness: We do not have a prayer house.

Procurator: You have a prayer house on Poklonnaya Hill. Why don't you go there? You're forbidden to meet in a private house.

Aida: Do you remember which other believers were fined?

Witness: I remember many believers were fined. When we were standing on the platform after the meeting . . .

Judge: Where was this?

Witness: I forget what the station was called; from the Finland Station you go . . . (*from the hall someone suggests Lavriki*). Yes, at Lavriki Station we were standing on the platform waiting for the train, when suddenly some auxiliary police came up and took several of us away. They fined them all.

Procurator: What were you doing on the platform?

Witness: We were standing waiting for a train. We were returning from a meeting.

Procurator: Where was the meeting held?

Witness: In the woods.

Procurator: It's forbidden to hold a service in a public place. That's why you were fined.

Witness: There was no one else in the woods, we were alone; we held our meeting and went away, but then some were picked up on the platform when we were already going home. Once the auxiliary police came to a meeting in Kuzmolovo. We met in Protsenko's house. They photographed us and then put the photographs up in the street. They photographed some drunks and put our photographs up beside theirs.

Judge: Defendant, do you have any further questions for the witness?

Aida: No.

Judge: Did you receive any presents from your foreign friends?

Aida: I'm surprised at this question. I've never heard that to give or receive presents is forbidden.

Judge: In the letter to Valya and Masha you write: "I've sent you a present on your release. It's from Margarita."

Aida: I sent Valya and Masha a New Testament, which Margarita had given me as a present.

[*The next witness to be questioned is called Ilyina. She is warned, like the other witnesses, about the penalty for giving*

false evidence. The Judge asks her whether she understands her responsibility, to which she answers:]
Witness: I understand, but I don't know why I was summoned. I haven't seen Skripnikova for five years. I don't remember anything, I could make a mistake. What can I say about her, I've forgotten everything. In 1963 I had concussion.
Judge: Have you known the accused long?
Witness: We lived together in the same hostel in 1962.
Judge: What can you say about Skripnikova?
Witness: Aida was a good person.
Judge: In what sense?
Witness: She wasn't malicious. If you asked her to do something she would help.
Judge: How many of you were there in the room?
Witness: Three: Limonnikova lived with us as well.
Judge: How did you get on?
Witness: Very well.
Judge: Here you are, the three of you, living in the same room: Limonnikova is an unbeliever, you're an unbeliever . . .
Witness: But I'm not an unbeliever.
Judge: You're a believer?
Witness: How can I put it: my mother is Orthodox and believes in God, but I'm uncommited.
Judge: Did you know Aida was a believer?
Witness: I knew that Aida was a believer, she explained it to us, but this didn't interest me much.
Judge: You knew how Aida came to be a believer.
Witness: I don't remember whether Aida told me herself or whether I heard it from others: at first she wasn't a believer, but then she began to believe after the death of her brother. I no longer remember anything exactly.
Judge: But look here, at the preliminary investigation you talked about Aida in detail.
Witness: At the preliminary investigation I said what I remembered, but the investigator wrote it down in his own way.
Judge: What do you mean? Did he not write down what you said?
Witness: Well, I don't know. We were just chatting and there were only the two of us.
Judge: But this is a different situation and you're getting flustered.

Witness: I haven't seen Aida for a long time now. It's difficult for me to remember everything.
Judge: What do you think: was Aida a very fervent believer then or not?
Witness: In my opinion not very.
Judge: What else can you remember?
Witness: Aida was convicted by a Comrades' Court because she distributed religious cards.[19] I wasn't at the Comrades' Court.
Judge: What is your opinion, was Aida a quiet person or did she like attention paid to her, did she like being in the public eye? What do you think?
Witness: I don't know, it's difficult for me to say. In my opinion, the Comrades' Court had a bad effect on Aida. I'm simply giving my own opinion. But it seems to me that Aida liked the attention which was paid to her and she became worse.
Judge: Did you know anything about Skripnikova's acquaintance with foreigners?
Witness: I heard that she had a friend in Sweden.
Procurator: How long did you live with Aida?
Witness: About a year.
Procurator: Was Aida persecuted for her belief?
Witness: No.

[*The last witness to enter the courtroom for questioning is a friend of Aida and also a believer. Her name is Ekaterina Andreyevna Boiko.*]

Judge: Do you know the defendant?
Witness: Yes.
Judge: Is Aida your friend?
Witness: Yes.
Judge: What can you say about her?
Witness: She's good and kind.
Judge: Is this all you can say about her? Aida is your friend, you know her well. Perhaps you can speak about her in more detail? What sort of character has she?
(*The witness remains silent*)
Judge: Tell us then when you met Aida.

19. This happened in April 1962. The poem which she distributed on post-cards is printed on p. 22.

Witness: I got to know Aida well after her release.
Judge: What did Aida do for a living?
Witness: After her release Aida got a job. She was soon sacked. After some time some policemen came to my place and asked for Aida. I wasn't at home. The neighbours said that they didn't know Aida and that she didn't live there. The police came several times. They told the neighbours that Aida didn't work and had no residence permit. Once a neighbour said to me: "Tell Aida not to come here." I asked: "Why?" She replied: "Aida's a spy." After Aida was sacked from the printing works, she began looking for a job. I sometimes went with her. Aida stopped looking for work in June (1967) when we discovered that they wanted to arrest her.
Judge: When the police came to you and started asking about Aida, did they tell you why they were interested in her?
Witness: The police came in my absence. They told the neighbours that Aida wasn't working and had no residence permit. The neighbours told me that they had sent for Aida – this must have been about June or July. At the preliminary investigation I said that I coudn't state the time exactly.
Judge: (to the defendant) The reason the police were interested in you was that you weren't working and had no residence permit. (To the witness) What money did Aida live on?
Witness: Ask her.
Judge: Did you ask Aida what money she lived on?
Witness: Once I asked her whether she had any money. She said that she had. But when I looked in her purse there was only one rouble there.
Judge: Did you help her on that occasion?
Witness: Myself, no.
Judge: But did you do something or tell others about it?

(*the witness remains silent*).

Procurator: Was your flat searched?
Witness: Yes.
Procurator: Was anything removed from your flat during the search?
Witness: Some magazines were removed from my flat. The *Herald of Salvation*.
Procurator: From whom did you receive these magazines?
Witness: I didn't receive them from Aida.

Procurator: What did you know about the visit of the Swedish tourists to Skripnikova?
Witness: I knew nothing about it. I found out about it the next day. The police called on Aida at the flat. I was at Aida's then. A policeman said that some literature, which Aida had given them, had been taken from some foreigners.
Judge: What sort of literature was this?
Witness: I don't know what it all was, but he took out of his folder the journal *Herald of Salvation, Fraternal Leaflet* and transcripts of trials. The policeman said that he knew that the foreigners had also handed over some literature, and he demanded that Aida should return it all. Aida said that she would do so. These were New Testaments.
Procurator: What sort of education have you had?
Witness: I reached the tenth class.
Procurator: Apart from religious literature, do you read anything else?
Witness: I read fiction as well.
Procurator: Why didn't you study any further?
Witness: I wanted to go to medical school, but in my character reference they wrote that I was a believer and a member of the schismatic Baptists, and so I didn't enter medical school. I would have been expelled in any case.
Procurator: And you didn't even try?
Witness: I knew from the example of others that they wouldn't let me study anyway.
Judge: Defendant, do you wish to question the witness?
Aida: Yes. Tell me, please, when the police called on you, did they only tell the neighbours that I wasn't working and had no residence permit, or did they mention the foreigners?
Judge: Defendant, you are not to ask questions in that form. You yourself are suggesting the answer.
Witness: My neighbours told me that Aida was meeting some foreigners. I remember it well.
Aida: In the summer of 1967, did you and I go to the legal advice bureau?
Witness: Yes.
Aida: Why did we go there?
Witness: To find out about a residence permit. When they began saying that Aida's residence permit had been withdrawn, Aida and I went to the legal advice bureau in order

to find out after what period they could cross a person off, if he doesn't live in the place inscribed in his residence permit.
Aida: What did they tell us?
Witness: They told us the law and showed us the article which said that if a person wasn't living in the place of his residence permit, then he can be crossed off after six months and no earlier. We were even told that if, after six months, one spends one night in the place of one's residence permit, then one needn't appear there again for six months and still won't be crossed off.
Judge: This law concerns a person with a residence permit giving him the right to living-space, but not a person who has registered without the right to living-space.
Aida: (to the witness) Do you know the name Tona from Sosnogorsk? (to the Judge) There's a letter of Tona's from Sosnogorsk amongst the evidence which is why I am asking her name.
Witness: Her surname is Khudyakova.
Aida: Can you name the believers whom they fined?
Witness: Maria Chendaruk, Sukovitsin, Lukas, Semenova and the Vezikovs.
Aida: What were they fined for?
Witness: For attending a prayer meeting.
Judge: Where did these meetings take place?
Witness: The prayer meetings took place in believers' homes and in the woods. I can tell you how they fined Maria Chendaruk. We were standing on the platform at Lavriki station waiting for the train. Suddenly some auxiliary policemen came up to us and took Chendaruk. We were standing beside her. I watched her being led away. They took her to the police station and fined her there.
Judge: Did they simply come up to her like that and take her off?
Witness: Yes. We were standing waiting for the train to Leningrad; the auxiliary police came up and took a number of us.
Judge: Why were you at Lavriki station?
Witness: We had been having a prayer meeting in the woods and when it was over we walked to the station and waited on the platform for the train.
Judge: Why do you hold prayer meetings in the woods? You have a prayer house at Poklonnaya Hill. Why don't you go

there?
Witness: Christ said that the time would come when people would not worship on the holy hill, but wherever a man called on the name of the Lord he would be saved.
Judge: Your community isn't registered. You hold prayer meetings in an unauthorized place, you disrupt public order – that's why you're fined.
Witness: We applied for registration. Our meeting disturbed no one in Lavriki.
Procurator: You know that every community must be registered?
Witness: Yes.
Procurator: Do you consider yourself a citizen of the Soviet Union?
Witness: Yes, I do.
Procurator: Do you consider yourself obliged to observe Soviet laws?
Witness: I do observe the laws.
Procurtor: You meet in Lukas's home and your community isn't registered.
Witness: The prayer meetings at Lukas's are not against the law. Lenin said: "Only in (Tsarist) Russia and in Turkey, out of all European states, were there still shameful laws against people of other beliefs."
Procurator: Where did you live before?
Witness: In the Komi Autonomous Republic in the town of Sosnogorsk.
Procurator: Are there believers there?
Witness: Yes. None of the communities is registered there.

A number of witnesses had not appeared in court, but, after consulting Aida, the court decides to continue with the trial in their absence. Aida at this point complains at the way the court has paid too much attention to irrelevant matters such as her manner of dress, her food, instead of concentrating on the actual indictment, i.e. that she spread false information about the church in Russia and thus slandered the Soviet state and social order.

Aida continues . . .

I wish to ask the court to pay a little more attention to the essential aspect of the case. For example, I would like to ex-

plain why our community is not registered. Tell me please, for breaking exactly which laws are we refused registration?
Judge: Defendant, the court asks you the questions, not you the court.
Procurator: I cannot understand what the defendant wants.
Aida: I am asking the court to pay more attention to the essential questions of the indictment, and ask that the piling-up of side issues should not obscure the essential aspect of the case for the court. This is my first petition. My second is to ask you, the court, to find out the exact date when my residence permit was removed.
Judge: Why do you need this?
Aida: I shall need this for my defence. I had a stamp for a permanent residence permit in my passport. No one has ever told me officially that I have been crossed off. There's not one scrap of paper about this matter. If they say I have no residence permit, then let them tell me the exact date on which my residence permit was cancelled.
Judge: The court cannot understand why you need to know when you were crossed off. Why do you need this for your defence? Explain, so that the court may understand.
Aida: In the legal proceedings they spoke about the fact that I wasn't working from 11 April 1967. I explained why I wasn't working. I wasn't working because since May 1967 criminal proceedings were being instituted against me and they were looking for me. Here they are trying to present the case as though the militia were looking for me, not because there were proceedings against me, but because I was not working and allegedly because I was without a residence permit. I wish to prove that this was not so. In the spring of 1967, proceedings were taken against a group of believers from our church. I was also included. They wanted to arrest me, but at that time I had just lost my job. If I had been working it would have been simple and easy to arrest me at work, but on this occasion they had to search for me. The militia first came to Boiko's flat on 4 May. I was sacked from my job at the printing works on 21 April, on the pretext of a reduction of staff. I began looking for work. From 21 April to 4 May is too short a period for the militia to become interested in why a person isn't working, all the more so if she is out of work through no fault of her own. As regards a resi-

dence permit, they couldn't cancel it before 4 May. On 17 February I was permanently and clearly registered and they couldn't possibly cross me off for two months. I suggest that this was done in July or August, but not in May, and certainly not before 4 May. My landlady only wrote to me in September. She wrote thus: "The Procurator's office has begun looking for you and the police have crossed you off." Up to this time I regularly sent money for the room. I am therefore asking the court to find out the exact date when they cancelled my residence permit, then it will be perfectly clear that the militia were searching for me not because of my work situation and residence permit, but because proceedings were already then being taken and that I did not think this up. I can even tell you why proceedings were started against me at that time. Twice in our prayer house I approached foreigners and asked them for a Bible. This became known to the authorities.

Judge: The question of a residence permit has nothing to do with the case. You're accused of distributing deliberately false statements slandering the Soviet state and social order.

Aida: But the question of work and a residence permit received a lot of attention in the judical proceedings.

Judge: These questions interested the court not because you are being charged with this, but because the court must assess your personality. It may seem strange to you that the court even asks about your character. The court must know what sort of person you are. In passing sentence the court takes the personality of the defendant into account.

Aida: In that case it is all the more necessary to grant my petition. The court must form an objective opinion about my personality.

Judge: Do you still have a petition?

Aida: Yes, I still have one important petition. I wish to summon Miss Jursmar as a witness. At the preliminary investigation I was shown Jursmar's notebook and was asked what the letters I.T. meant. I said that I didn't know; it was difficult for me to make it out in someone else's notebook. I was not asked any more questions about Jursmar's notebook. However, yesterday in the judicial proceedings, Jursmar's notebook was the centre of attention. It was even alleged that Jursmar and I had almost formed a conspiracy. I wish to summon Jursmar to court, so that she herself can explain her notes and say for whom the *Herald of Salvation* and the *Fraternal Leaflets* were intended: for the BBC, for the Voice of America or for believers. If it is difficult to summon Jursmar to court, then one could write to the Swedish authorities asking them to question Jursmar on these points, just as, for example, they wrote to Magnitogorsk asking them to question my sister.

Judge: This is a serious petition. We shall discuss it. What is your opinion, Mr. Procurator, with regard to this petition by the defendant?

Procurator: Regarding the first petition by the defendant, this is not a petition, but simply dissatisfaction with the course of the trial. Clearly she would like to turn the trial into a forum for propagating or reading anti-Soviet literature. If Skripnikova considers that something has not been elucidated, she can write a memorandum for the judicial enquiry. Skripnikova's second petition is connected with her residence permit. I consider that this question has no significance with regard to the charge as stated. But I leave this question to be examined by the court. I also leave Skripnikova's third petition to be examined by the court. As for Skripnikova's request to summon Jursmar to court, as a witness, this petition cannot be carried out in practice. Jursmar is a foreign subject. Soviet jurisdiction does not extend to her. If Jursmar was in the territory of the USSR, we could make her appear in court, but we cannot summon her from Sweden, nor send a separate request that Jursmar be questioned.

Judge: What is your opinion, defendant?

Aida: If my petition to summon Jursmar to court cannot be carried out in practice, then I don't insist on it. But in that case it will be difficult to make out what is written in Jursmar's notebook. I ask the court to comply with my petition to find out the exact date when I lost my residence permit and to find the article in the Civil Code concerning the question of a residence permit.

Judge: After consultation the court has resolved that the defendant's petitions be turned down.

The Procurator then draws the attention of the court to the verdict given at the trial of the Baptist F.B. Makhovitsky in Leningrad on 25-28 November 1966 at the Kirov district court, and to the verdict given at the trial of the Baptists Lukas, Zhukova and Semenova at the Leningrad city court. They were all accused of breaking Soviet legislation on the separation of church and state and of schools from the church and sentenced under Article 142 of the RSFSR Criminal Code. It appears that the Procurator considers Aida also guilty of breaking this article of the Criminal Code, because she belonged to an unregistered Baptist community.

Judge: Defendant Skripnikova, you don't object to this material being filed?

Aida: No, I don't object, but I request the opportunity to familiarize myself with it.

Judge: Would you like it now or during the adjournment?

Aida: During the adjournment.

Judge: Yesterday you told a lie. You said that the participation of a lawyer in the trial did not go against your religious convictions, but in Valya and Masha's letter you yourself write: "Three of us have been tried: Pavel Lukas, Valya Zhukova, Lida Semenova. Lida's father hired a lawyer, and in order not to offend her father, Lida did not refuse the lawyer. She felt slightly uncomfortable because all believers usually refuse a lawyer." Doesn't this mean that the participation of a lawyer in the trial goes against your religious convictions?

Aida: No, believers refuse lawyers because lawyers don't defend them. Why should I have a third accuser here?

Judge: There will be an adjournment for an hour.

After the adjournment

Procurator: Defendant, tell us how many members there are in your community?

Aida: I cannot tell you exactly. There must be about two hundred.

Procurator: You know the laws which regulate the relationship between believers and the state?

Aida: Yes, I know the Decree on the separation of the church from the state and of schools from the church.

Procurator: You know the rule for the registration of communities?

Aida: Yes, the community hands in an application and indicates what it is organized for. The authorities are obliged to

register a community if the aims of the community do not contradict the law.
Judge: Did the search of your room[20] happen in your presence?
Aida: Yes.
Judge: After the search of your room many illegal publications of the CCECB and a number of copies of several publications were taken away. For example, two or three copies of some issues of the *Herald of Salvation*. Why did you need several numbers of one and the same journal?
Aida: I always tried to take a few more copies of the *Herald of Salvation* in order to distribute them to my friends, because I myself love this journal.
Judge: The judicial enquiry is finished. Let us pass on to the speeches of the two parties. Leave is now given to Procurator Timofeeva to proceed for the prosecution.

The Procurator's speech

Before I speak about the defendant, I wish to speak about the history of the Church of Evangelical Christians and Baptists (ECB) in Russia. The first communities of Evangelical Christians and Baptists appeared in Russia 100 years ago. In the beginning communities of Baptists and Evangelical Christians were formed in St. Petersburg, in the Ukraine and in the Caucasus, but gradually the new teaching spread into the depths of Russia. The state religion in Tsarist Russia was the Orthodox faith and all other faiths were forbidden. The Orthodox Church occupied the dominant position. After the Great October Socialist Revolution in our country the Church was separated from the state and believers of all faiths received the right to freedom of belief.

In 1944 the communities of Evangelical Christians and the communities of Baptists united and a governing body was set up – the All-Union Council of Evangelical Christians and Baptists – the AUCECB.

The achievements of socialist construction undermined the social roots of religion and promoted the mass secession of believers from religion. Church people had to adapt themselves in order to hold on to believers.

20. This happened on 12 April, 1968.

In 1961 there was a schism in the ECB Church. The so-called Action Group accused the AUCECB of deviating from doctrinal norms and conducted a struggle for the removal of the AUCECB from the leadership. Later the Action Group was called the Organizing Committee and then the Council of Churches. The Council of Churches drew some believers onto its side; this was an insignificant proportion.[21] Taking refuge in religious dogma, the Council of Churches is fighting in fact for a change in the legislation on religious cults.[22] The Council of Churches in its letters and appeals calls on believers not to submit to the law. The communities which support the Council of Churches are breaking the legislation relating to cults. These communities are not registered,[23] their meetings take place in private homes and in public places. Some believers were convicted for breaking the legislation on cults. The Council of Churches presents this as persecution for the faith. For seven years already the Council of Churches has been carrying on this titanic struggle with the authorities. This struggle has had various stages. At present the Council of Churches is attempting to appeal to foreign countries in order to rouse public opinion there.

The defendant, Skripnikova, is a member of the unregistered Leningrad ECB community which belongs to the Council of Churches. There are many addresses from various cities in the Soviet Union and abroad in Skripnikova's notebook. This is evidence that Skripnikova had links throughout the country, but her main task was to organize contacts abroad. It must be said that she measured up to this task well. It is not by chance that Skripnikova wanted so much to live in Leningrad itself. Many foreigners come there and it is the most convenient place for making contacts. I do not know why the police gave her a residence permit. I consider that such a person ought not to have one.

21. The support for the CCECB was probably much greater than implied by these words.
22. This refers to the reformers' demand for changes in the 1929 *Laws on Religious Associations*, which in many ways contradicted the guarantee of freedom of conscience in the Constitution and the 1918 Decree on separation of church and state.
23. Many of these communities had in fact applied for registration, but had been refused it and then met in private.

Long ago Aida attracted the attention of the organs of the State security. Already in 1958 she wrote an anti-Soviet letter to the editor of *Pravda.* Several public organizations in Leningrad have had much to do with Aida. On the decision of the Comrades' Court she was given a job in a laboratory which did not correspond to her qualifications. She was helped in her studies. Aida's life began unfortunately in that she was born into a family of Baptists. Of coure it's a pity that we let a person slip away, but we talked a lot to Aida and made the anti-social character of her actions clear. Skripnikova's education has gone only up to the eighth class. This is of course very little, though she is intelligent and capable. I don't know why she didn't complete studying at the technical school and left in the first year. I think she had the ability to finish the technical school course. Skripnikova distributed copies of the *Herald of Salvation* and other illegal publications of the Council of Churches. These publications contained deliberately false statements, slandering the Soviet state and social order.

For example in the *Herald of Salvation* No. 19, there is the article "A century's path of struggle and suffering". I think that the defendant wrote this article herself. Of course she didn't write it alone, but together with others. This article talks of believers being persecuted; that they are not allowed to study, that they are dismissed from their jobs, that they are fined and tried because of their belief. Kryuchkov said at his trial in Moscow: "Those brothers who are in prisons and camps do not suffer because they have broken Soviet laws; they suffer because they have remained faithful to the Lord." All this is a deliberately false statement which slanders the Soviet state and social order. In the Soviet Union there are various faiths, churches are open and no one is persecuted for his faith. The State does not interfere in the activities of religious bodies, if these communities do not break the legislation on cults. The defendant Skripnikova's guilt of systematically distributing false statements which slander the Soviet state and social order is fully proved. These actions are rightly covered by article 190/1 of the Criminal Code of the RSFSR. I request the court, according to article 190/1, to sentence the defendant, Skripnikova, to two and a half years of imprisonment.

Aida Skripnikova's defence speech

I was intending to speak on the substance of the charge brought against me, but other questions have been touched on here, so I must also deal with them, although, as has been said, they have no connection with this case. The Procurator said that in 1958 I wrote a letter of anti-Soviet content to the editor of *Pravda.* In 1958, you will remember, the newspapers were fulminating against Pasternak for his *Doctor Zhivago.* At that time many critics were writing condemning Pasternak. I also wrote. I wrote that I didn't understand how it was possible to condemn Pasternak, if no one had read his novel. You shouldn't condemn something you don't know.

The Procurator says that I got a job in a laboratory thanks to society, following the decision of the Comrades' Court. This does not fit the facts. It happened like this: I got a job in a construction firm, No. 16. After four months I discovered from a certain woman that they needed an assistant in the firm's laboratory. The work there was simple and did not require any qualifications or special training. I went to the laboratory, spoke to the head, who said she would take me on, I liked the work and took the job there. I got the job myself, without any patronage. I'm telling you what happened. If you look carefully at the case materials you will be convinced of this. In the dossier there's a statement from the Museum of Religion and Atheism about the work for re-educating me, which I was given. The statement says that I was given a job in the laboratory following the decision of the Comrades' Court, but I began work in the laboratory in February 1961, whereas the Comrades' Court sat in April 1962. But that's not all. In the dossier there's the verbatim report of the Comrades' Court. If you look at it you'll see that the resolution of the Comrades' Court was precisely to transfer me from the laboratory to work in a construction team. They knew that I liked the work and wanted to punish me somehow. But then there was some disagreement amongst them; some said I should be transferred, others said I should not, and while they were arguing, I worked three years in the laboratory. No criticisms were made about me at work, but for three years the threat of dismissal hung over me. Apart from me, there were six other people working in the laboratory; why did they have more right to work than I?

Now I will tell you how I was sacked from the printing works. This does have a certain bearing on the case, because when I say I was dismissed from my work for my faith, I am told, "That is a deliberately false statement." After my release from prison I was registered outside the city – I was registered permanently in Volkhovstroye. I found work in a printing works. A week after starting work I was at a prayer meeting. The police arrived and took down my name, along with several others. A policeman took my identity document and copied out from it the place of my résidence permit. I knew that they would report me to my place of work. I had only been working five days and they did not know at work that I was a believer. The next day I told the shift foreman that the police would phone, because they had taken my name at a prayer meeting. Then the shift foreman told me that they had been phoning and were coming. I myself did not see anyone, but this is what the shift foreman told me. Everyone at the printing works got alarmed when they found out that I was a believer, and began to chat to me. The secretary of the party organization chatted to me several times. She advised me to renounce my faith and said that I would then be sent on a proof-reading course; "our society is a humanitarian one", etc. But right from the start, they did not hide from me the fact that if I did not change my views, I would be sacked. They told me straight out. "The printing works is a political institution; not everybody can work here," although this printing works was under the management of the railways and nothing secret was printed there – only forms of all sorts, boarding permits and train timetables. I don't know what there was there which I couldn't be trusted with. Things went on like this for three weeks. Then the shift foreman told me that a management commission was due to arrive to discuss production, and they would settle my question at the same time. The following day the commission arrived and a day later I was summoned to the manager and told that I'd been dismissed. Of course they didn't say that they were dismissing me because of my faith, because there is no such law that people can be dismissed for their faith, so they sacked me on the pretext of a staff reduction. When I went to the shop-floor and said that I had been dismissed due to a staff reduction, the workers' eyes nearly popped out of their heads. One of the machines had been standing idle because there was no one to work on it.

After being sacked I started to look for work. I soon found a job. They promised to take me on at one particular factory, so I began to fill in the necessary forms. Then in the personnel department I was given a sheet of paper on which I had to sign a pledge not to disclose production secrets. This surprised me and I decided that I ought to talk everything over immediately. If they had dismissed me from a simple printing works, they were even more likely to dismiss me from a factory where there were production secrets. I told them that I was a believer, that I'd been dismissed from a printing works, and told them to decide straight away whether or not to take me on, so that they would not have to sack me in a month's time due to a staff reduction. The woman who was attending to me asked me to wait a moment, and went off to the manager. About fifteen minutes later she returned and said, "We can't engage you because your permit is valid only outside the city." As if they hadn't previously seen that I had a non-city residence permit; as if the manager hadn't previously looked at my papers.

I began to look for work again and had already got a job as an orderly in a home for the disabled and even worked there for one day, although I was not yet officially registered but I had to leave there too – and here's the reason why. It was the middle of June, and about this time it became clear even to me that I would be arrested. From 4 May onwards the police began to look for me. They went to the flats of believers and questioned neighbours. To begin with I didn't attribute any significance to this, thinking they intended only to warn me not to approach any foreigners in the prayer house. I therefore disregarded the fact that the police were looking for me and got on with my own business – finding work. But then they started asking questions about me in the Procurator's office. Searches were carried out in believers' flats and many of them began to be summoned to this office. We knew that a case was being compiled on a group of believers. From the questions asked at the Procurator's office we could surmise whom they wanted to try. When it became apparent that I was among them, I didn't attempt to register for work, because they would have arrested me immediately.

Only six months had elapsed since my release and I wanted to do something useful before going to prison again. I had work which I had to finish.

(At this point Aida asked for a break of ten minutes)

Now I will speak specifically on the substance of the charge brought against me. I am charged under Article 190/1 of the RSFSR Criminal Code, which reads: "The systematic distribution of deliberately false statements, slandering the Soviet state and social order." I am charged with the distribution of the journals *Herald of Salvation* and *Fraternal Leaflet*, and transcripts of trials, which are supposed to contain delibertely false statements slandering the Soviet state and social order. I am charged with distributing literature to four people in different places: to Miss Jursmar of Stockholm, Zinaida Skripnikova of Magnitogorsk, Shishkini of the Kirov region and David from Sweden. I do not deny these facts. The prosecution has no proof that I sent literature anywhere else, but I won't say anything about that.

The distribution of any publication is not in itself a crime and if the prosecution hadn't found any deliberately false statements in the magazines *Herald of Salvation* and *Fraternal Leaflet* there would be no grounds on which to try me. Therefore I must talk about the contents of this literature.

I must bring in a bit of history. I shall not talk about the distant past, only from 1961 on. The Procurator maintains that the Council of Churches and the communities which support it are struggling against the authorities and breaking the law. In 1961 an Action Group composed of ministers of the church was formed.[24] I'm not going to talk about the activities of this Action Group or about why it broke away from the registered communities. Those are internal Church affairs and should not be discussed here. I shall merely say how the activity of the Action Group appears in relation to the state. The Action Group addressed a letter to all believers, in which the position of the church was explained and the calling of a congress proposed. Simultaneously the Action Group sent a letter to the authorities asking permission to hold a congress. These actions in no way contravene the law. The authorities should have given permission for the congress. Incidentally,

24. See Chapter II *The Background.*

in the Law of 1929 it says that believers have the right to organize congresses. But instead of giving permission, the authorities began to persecute those who had asked for the congress and prosecuted many of them. Here they say that the believers were tried not for their faith but for anti-social activity and that from 1961 the activities of the Action Group have been of an unlawful nature. But the prosecution passes over in silence the fact that in 1964-65 150 believers sentenced in 1961-63 were rehabilitated. Obviously this silence is not accidental. Rehabilitation is not the same as a reprieve or an amnesty; rehabilitation means that a man is recognized as not guilty.

In March 1966 the decree[25] enforcing article 142 of the Criminal Code of the RSFSR was passed, whereupon trials of believers were again instigated.

The magazine *Herald of Salvation* is a religious magazine. *Fraternal Leaflet* is published by the Council of Churches as an information leaflet. As I am charged with the distribution of this literature, I shall have to speak in detail about its contents. The investigator noted down seventeen "seditious" phrases out of all the literature. This was during interrogation on 5 June; in the dossier there is the report of the interrogation, and these seventeen phrases, according to the investigator, contain deliberately false statements, slandering the Soviet state and social order. I must say something about the articles from which these phrases are taken and read out certain phrases in context. Here are three phrases which the investigator noted down from *Herald of Salvation* No. 19:

1. "Atheism, having become the state religion in our land, began to persecute believers as zealously as the Orthodox clergy had done at the time of the autocracy, counting them as lambs for the slaughter."
2. "In their places of work, study and residence believers are subjected to varying methods of re-education, to threats, exclusion from educational institution, dismissal from work, etc."

25. The text of this decree is contained in Michael Bourdeaux, *Religious Ferment in Russia*, London, 1968, pp. 159–160. This decree listed various types of activity punishable under article 142, and may well have been aimed specifically at the reform Baptists.

3. "In March 1966 decrees directed against unregistered communities were published, with the aim of suppressing spiritual revival."

These sentences are taken from the article "A century's path of struggle and suffering". The *Herald of Salvation* No. 19 was a jubilee issue. In 1967 one hundred years had passed since the Evangelical Church arose in Russia and *Herald of Salvation* No. 19 was devoted to this century. "A century's path of struggle and suffering" is an historical article in which the life of the church over the past one hundred years is recounted. When writing history one must write about things as they were, without falsification. In the *Herald of Salvation* No. 19 the history of the church is recounted accurately. Things are recorded as they actually were. This wasn't written because someone was inimicably disposed towards the Soviet authorities. I'll read out a description of the life of the church in Tsarist times:

"Neither fearing the Tsar's laws forbidding the preaching of the Gospel, nor dismayed by the *pogroms* carried out by whole crowds of the people stirred up by the Orthodox priests, the first witnesses to Christ in our country expressed His teaching. They endured the kind of persecution which only man's wickedness could devise."

"But from the very first moments of life of the Church of Christ in Russia, the enemy of human souls unleashed upon it harsh persecution, in response to its desire to live a new devout life. In the life of the Church, the period of 1867-1905 could be called the period of the deprivation of rights and of persecution."

"The church and secular press did not shun any falsehood in presenting the life of the Stundists[26] in the worst possible light."

"In the years 1912-1913 circulars limiting the freedom of religion were issued by the government."

This refers to Tsarist times. This persecution is described in even stronger colours than the persecution under the Soviet regime. From 1867 to 1905 there was persecution and this fact is not disregarded in the article. From 1905 to 1914 there was freedom, and this too is stated. I'll read on: "Between

26. An early name for the Evangelicals in Russia.

1914 and 1917 followers of Evangelical Baptist teaching were again subjected to persecution. All their places of worship were closed in St. Peterburg."

"But God set a limit on these persecutions, too. Religious freedom was proclaimed in a decree of the Soviet government – *On the separation of Church and State, and of Schools from the Church.* Based on this decree, the thirteenth article of the Constitution concerning freedom of conscience recognized the freedom of religious and anti-religious propaganda for all citizens. This is why the 1920s were years of favourable opportunities in the life of our fellowship." In the 1920s there was religious freedom. The believers carried on their public worship in freedom.

Witness Boiko began to quote Lenin; I'll complete the quotation: "Only in Russia and Turkey were shameful laws against religious people still in force. These laws either directly prohibited the open profession of faith or forbade its propagation. These laws are the most unjust, shameful and oppressive." I should like to draw your attention to the word "propagation". Lenin called the prohibition on the propagation of the faith unjust and shameful. In the 1920s there was freedom for missionary activities; preachers were able to travel about the whole country and organize missionary meetings; the state did not interfere in internal church affairs. Christian parents were free to bring up their own children themselves. In the decree "On the separation of Church and State" it says, "Citizens may give and receive instruction in private." In those days this was taken literally, so that believers were permitted to open private Sunday schools, and these were opened in many parishes. There was no persecution in the 1920s – indeed no one says that there was. And in the article life is recorded as it was. In the 1920s the Soviet authorities were already in power. In "A century's path of struggle and suffering" the Church's history is written objectively. And if the article talks about persecution, this isn't with the aim of slandering the Soviet authorities; there are no bad intentions here.

Now I can analyze these three sentences which the investigator took from the article "A century's path of struggle and suffering", to see whether what is said in them corresponds to reality.

1. Atheism, having become the state religion in our land, began to persecute believers as zealously as the Orthodox clergy had done at the time of the autocracy, counting them as "lambs for the slaughter." Here the writers have in mind the 1930s.[27] This can be seen from the text of the article, because there the description follows a chronological order. Well, what can one say about the 1930s? Does much need to be said? Everyone knows what they were like. I don't think even the most ardent atheist would dare say that there was no persecution of believers during those years. It's said that at one point even Christmas trees were forbidden because they were regarded as a reminder of religion. And if such a distant, dead reminder of religion was banned, one can imagine the fate of living witnesses to the faith. Sometimes within the space of one night half the members of one community would disappear. Thus there is no deliberately false statement in this sentence. Everyone knows what things were like in the 1930s.

The next sentence reads: "In their places of work, study and residence believers are subjected to varying methods of re-education, to threats, exclusion from educational institutes, dismissal from work, etc." Dismissal from work and exclusion from educational institutions were applied with particular severity in 1956 and the years 1958-62. Now this happens less frequently, as far as I know. But I don't know exactly. It's impossible to talk about the history of our church without mentioning dismissal from work and exclusion from educational institutions, because believers have experienced these things and they have been quite widespread. I can quote certain facts. For example, Josif Bondarenko from Odessa was barred from a shipbuilding institute in 1962; he was not allowed to defend his diploma. I've already told you how I was sacked from the printing works. In the autumn of 1963 Nadezhda Ivanovna Vins[28] was sacked. She used to work in a school teaching English and was mentioned in the list of the city's best teachers, but when her husband was written about in the papers she was immediately sacked.

The third sentence reads: "In March 1966 decrees directed against unregistered communities were published, with the aim of suppressing spiritual revival." Following the decree of 18

27. These were the most oppressive years of Stalin's dictatorship.
28. The wife of Georgi Vins, leader of the reform Baptists.

March on the enforcement of Article 142 of the Criminal Code of the RSFSR, persecution and arrests began anew, and again many believers were convicted. This is a fact, not a deliberately false statement. "We report that fines, *pogroms*, searches, trials and shadowing of members of the awakened Church continue in every area." The investigator noted this down from the *Herald of Salvation* No. 12, 1966. Trials of believers do take place; in more than 200 cases believers have been convicted. Believers are also shadowed. I will tell you how I was arrested. On 11 April I went to a prayer meeting. After the meeting, when we were returning home, we noticed that a man was looking at me very closely. From the meeting we all take the No. 32 bus as far as the terminus. There all the believers get out and some go to the No. 37 bus stop, others to the tram stop. Here too there was a shadow stationed, to see which believers were going to the prayer meeting. We noticed that I was being followed but I didn't attach any importance to this. The next day they came to my flat and arrested me. Searches are also frequently carried out at believers' homes. In connection with my case alone there were eleven searches: three in Leningrad, four in Perm, three in Znamenka, Kirovograd region, and one at my sister's home in Magnitogorsk. One can more or less understand the search at my flat and at Skurlova's and my sister's. But why make searches at other believers' places? They were only made because these addresses were found in my notebook. Nowhere did they find anything connected with my case. During the search of my room they found the address of the believers Dibrivnoi from Znamenka in Kirovograd region. The Leningrad Procurator's office sent an order for a search to be made at the Dibrivnoi's house and decided to seize this opportunity of making searches at the homes of other believers. A letter like this was sent from the Znamenka Procurator's office to Leningrad, along with the record of the interrogations and searches: "I must report that on our own initiative two searches were carried out at the homes of the Evangelical Baptist believers, N. B. Vdovchenko and G. Ya. Lunyachenko, and the religious literature removed from them is at the KGB office." Twenty-six tapes with recordings of sermons and hymns were taken from the Dibrivnois' place.

As far as fines are concerned, believers have been fined so

much that if all this money were collected up, a space-ship could probably be built with it. Witnesses Boiko and Skurlova gave the surnames of believers who have been fined for attending prayer meetings. Maya Chendaruk was fined 20 roubles for attending a meeting at Lavriki. Lukas, the Vezinovois, Sukovitsyn and Semenova were fined and I know that Protsenko was fined. Prayer meetings take place at home and don't disturb anyone. If they take place in the woods they don't disturb anyone either. In 1965 we met in the woods all summer and didn't disturb anyone, and no one disturbed us there, until the police began to come out and break up the meetings.

I don't know how prayer meetings can be called illegal, after all they take place every day. We believers can account for the persecutions, but how can atheists possibly explain the breaking up of the meetings rationally to themselves? I should find it difficult in their position.

"The Organizing Committee has made continual petitions for the liberation of Evangelical Christian and Baptist believers, convicted because of their faith in God, and also for the termination of persecution of ECB believers in our country." When I asked the investigator why he had picked this out and what he found deliberately false about this – for the Organizing Committee did indeed petition for the liberation of prisoners – he replied, "In the Soviet Union we don't try people for their faith, but you write 'prisoners are tried for their faith'; that is a deliberately false statement." Here is another passage also selected by the investigator as anti-Soviet:

> "Many church ministers who showed faithful and indefatigable concern for the church's purity and that it should walk in the light before the Lord, have been taken from us and sent off to prisons and camps."

I don't think it's necessary to read out all the sentences noted down by the investigator, as they are all about the same thing – trials, arrests, persecution and oppression in general. It's just these passges which the investigator picked out from the magazines *Herald of Salvation* and *Fraternal Leaflet.* And all these are called deliberately false statements.

The investigator picked three sentences from the legal proceedings against Vins and Kryuchkov:

"I must make it clear that the present case is a complete

fabrication. I have been arrested as a minister of the Church." This was stated by Vins during the trial.

"Those brethren at present in prisons and camps are suffering not because they have broken Soviet laws, but because they have maintained their loyalty to the Lord and to His Church."
Kryuchkov stated this in his final speech. I don't know, either, why these sentences are interpreted as deliberately false, because you (the court) do not say: Vins and Kryuchkov didn't state this, you made it up yourself. No, once again you say, "No one is tried for his faith in the Soviet Union, the Vins Kryuchkov case confirms it, therefore these are deliberately false statements." I fail to see how such an interpretation is possible. The report of a trial is the transcript of what was said during it. We record the Procurator's speech, although we don't agree with what he said.

And now the question arises about what we are being prosecuted for. We say, for our faith, but are told, "That's a deliberately false statement; you're being tried for infringing Soviet law." I'm a member of an unregistered community, which requested registration and put in an application. In the application the purpose for which the society is being organized is indicated; its aims and purposes are enumerated. The authorities take this application and if any of the society's proposed aims contravenes the law they tell the society about this, specifically, pointing out which particular law it's infringing. All our communities have sent in these applications, which include our statutes. We're not told, "You mustn't do this or that, it's against the law." Instead we're told, "Sign a pledge that you won't break the law." This isn't the correct procedure for registration.

During the court sitting I have tried to explain why I belong to an unregistered community. Just which law is our community breaking, so that it can't be registered? I haven't received any definite answer. However, here they've been saying that our community is breaking the law by attracting children and by refusing to recognize the ban on missionary activity. They tell us that we have freedom of religion, yet we seem to break the law on purpose – as if we were such malicious citizens that we spend our time thinking how to annoy the Soviet authorities. But believers can't promise to fulfil a law which forbids them to talk about God and forbids parents to bring up their children in the faith. For all their loyalty to the authorities, believers won't subscribe to such a law. No Christian mother or father will accept a law which orders them to bring up their children as atheists. They would rather go through whatever sufferings you like, rather stand in the dock, than promise to abide by this law. Of course there are parents for whom their faith is of secondary importance, although they call themselves believers; it's all the same to them what they promise. But those who really believe will break this law.

Christ said, "Preach the Gospel to every creature", and believers can't submit to a law forbidding them to talk about God and about salvation. Not a single believer will do this. Even if he's not a missionary or a preacher, even if he's incapable of preaching a sermon, it makes no difference – he won't submit to such a law, because even a person incapable of preaching a sermon will sometimes be able to tell someone about salvation. Therefore believers won't promise to carry out such a law. Despite all their respect for the authorities, they'll break this law. There are believers sitting here in this courtroom. Are they really such embittered people? Look at them. The majority of them are simple working men and women, very quiet and peaceable people. Why then do they break the law? Surely you can't think they enjoy simply enduring oppression like that, or that they are bad citizens, set against the authorities. No, I'll repeat it once more, believers can't keep a law which forces them to deny the Gospel. When we're tried for breaking such laws, we're quite justified in saying that we're being tried for our faith.

We are not at all demanding. It's said that in Sweden believers have beautiful places of worship, equipped with every amenity, but we're not used to this. At the end of 1964 and in 1965 our prisoners were rehabilitated and the police stopped breaking up our meetings. As we had no places of worship, we met in the woods and wherever we could, but we weren't prevented from holding our meetings. And for us, this is freedom. In conversation, if we recall some event or other, we sometimes say, "That was when we were free." We wouldn't say we were persecuted if it weren't true. What good would it do us to invent persecutions? Surely you don't think

I'd want to end up in prison for slandering the Soviet authorities? Persecution exists, that's a fact; but now I want to explain why this fact is talked about, why persecution is written about in the magazines and *Fraternal Leaflet.*

The investigator took the following sentence from *Fraternal Leaflet* No. 6 for 1966:

"In order to legalize illegalities committed against believers, the supreme authorities of our country passed a decree on 18 March 1966, by which people could be tried and fined for praying."

Why did the Council of Churches need to write that? Maybe the Council of Churches wants to say to believers, "Look how awful the Soviet authorities are"? Or had the Council of Churches some other motivation for writing those words? The sixth *Fraternal Leaflet* for 1966 was the June issue. What was June 1966 like for our Church? On 17 May 1966 a delegation of believers was arrested just outside the Central Committee building of the Communist Party. When persecutions and arrests started up again after the March decree, believers from all parts of the country gathered and came to Moscow to petition the government on behalf of our prisoners and to tell them about the persecutions, and this delegation was arrested, four hundred people at one go. Apart from this, almost the whole leadership of the Council of Churches was arrested in May. This was a terrible blow for the Church. Many believers were alarmed, and so in this complex situation the ministers of the Council of Churches wrote to believers in this *Fraternal Leaflet*. I'll read you the opening paragraphs of *Leaflet* No. 6:

"Let the groaning of the prisoner come before Thy face, and by the might of Thy right hand save those who are counted as sheep for the slaughter. Beloved, first of all we express our deep sorrow, in which we want to take comfort in the Lord and comfort all who share it with us. The Lord has led many of our ministers, including members of the CCECB which you elected, and also several sisters, along the way of prison and camps, for His glory. . . .

To be comforted we need to understand the causes and the reason for our sufferings, praying to God and carrying out His will. In order to legalize illegalities committed against believers the supreme authorities of our country passed a decree on 18 March 1966, by which people could be tried and fined for the open profession of their faith, for worshipping God and praying, as it was in the time of Daniel and Mordecai, of Christ and the Apostles. Like Daniel and the Apostles, the faithful carried on their service, regardless of threats, decrees, burning fiery furnaces, roaring lions, crosses and prisons, but cried to God. . . ."

What do you hear in these words? Bitterness towards the authorities? I can hear only grief and weeping. The ministers of the Council of Churches are sharing the sorrow of the Church, and want to comfort the believers. The organizational work of the Council of Churches is only a small part of its activities. Its members are spiritual ministers and as true ministers of the Church they share all its sorrows and sufferings and encourage and comfort the believers. Notice that the sentence: "In order to legalize illegalities committed against believers the supreme authorities of our country passed a decree on 18 March 1966, by which people could be tried and fined for the open profession of their faith, for worshipping God and praying" is followed by these words: ". . . as it was in the time of Daniel and Mordecai, of Christ and the Apostles". The words, "as it was", are extremely significant. Here the ministers of the Council of Churches are implying: do not be troubled, because cruel persecutions beset us. Believers of other times have already gone through all this; there were also decrees then. Let us be courageous, like Daniel and Mordecai and the Apostles; let us continue to serve God.

People have told me – I was in prison at the time – people have told me that, after the mass arrest, all the believers were alarmed, and *Fraternal Leaflet* No. 6 says just what the believers needed to be told at that time. One believer told me that *Fraternal Leaflet* brought her peace and encouragement; it was especially welcome in those days. When the Council of Churches writes about persecution, it's not in order to slander the state, but because its ministers, as spiritual pastors, are bound to care about the state of the church and support the believers at a difficult time. The *Fraternal Leaflets* in which persecutions are mentioned, do not end with a rallying-call against the state, nor do they incite readers to disobey the state; they end with exhortations to the believers to continue faithful to the Lord.

Now it remains only for me to tell you why I sent my friends the magazines and *Fraternal Leaflets.* Although I'm charged with distributing *Herald of Salvation* and other publications both abroad and in this country, during the court-sitting, I've been blamed most strongly for sending them abroad, so I'll tell you why I did this. I must make it clear that no one ordered me to send the magazines and *Fraternal Leaflets* abroad. I acted on my own initiative. For instance, at church they didn't find out till later that I had given Miss Jursmar literature. This was when I received visits from the police. I tried not to talk it over with anyone, so as to answer for everything alone. I know that *Herald of Salvation* and *Fraternal Leaflet* do not contain any deliberately false statements, but at the same time I know what it means to send them abroad. I knew that it could bring me into the dock.

In atheist literature the church is portrayed as consisting solely of leaders and their meek subordinates. The leaders give orders which their subordinates carry out, ready to rush blindly wherever they are told. This is completely untrue. I don't know a more democratic organization than the Church. All compulsion is excluded from it. I'm firmly convinced that every believer can find work to do in the church. Anyone who wants to work can find work suited to his strength and abilities. Absolutely everyone can be useful in the church. Believers often display their own initiative and do things of their own accord. Of course, there are also church standing orders, but in these no one forces anyone to do anything. Everything is done voluntarily. If a person doesn't want to do something, no one compels him to. The Procurator says that I have links throughout the country and abroad. People say this because they don't understand the structure of the church. No one in the church could have ordered me to dispatch the *Herald of Salvation* abroad, because that's very dangerous, and no one would suggest that I should expose myself to such danger. This could only be a question of individual initiative. I can ask one of the believers to do something, but I'd never ask anyone to go and send a *Herald of Salvation* abroad instead of me. I know it's dangerous, that's why I do it myself. And every believer would argue the same way. Each one will expose himself to danger before anyone else.

I didn't send *Herald of Salvation* and *Fraternal Leaflet* abroad because I'm ill-disposed towards the authorities. I'm an enthusiastic reader of *Herald of Salvation.* I sent this and *Fraternal Leaflet* abroad so that our brothers and sisters in the faith could find out about the life of the Russian Church. I love the Russian Church; it follows such a glorious path.

The Action Group, our movement within the church, is called various different things. Some call it a schism, but it's more correct to call it an awakening. Yes, it is an awakening, and it hit me. Faith was growing weak and suddenly there came an awakening. What I saw was quite miraculous. I saw the dead rising again – the spiritually dead, the weak proved capable of great feats. Once I was attracted by impressive external greatness, but then I came to know the greatness of humility and patience, the kind of greatness of the church's struggle. This revival quickened my spirit, too, and from that time onwards I have not been able to remain uninvolved. *Herald of Salvation* and *Fraternal Leaflet* give an account of the life of the awakened church. I wanted everyone to know about the awakening, and that's why I sent the magazines to my friends abroad. I gave Miss Jursmar the transcripts of the trials in Moscow and Ryazan for a different purpose from the magazines, although of course trials are part of the life of our church and it is impossible not to mention them in talking about the Russian Church. However, in handing over the transcripts of the trials to Miss Jursmar I was not only bearing this in mind, but something else as well. I was thinking that maybe they could somehow be used in petitioning on behalf of the prisoners unjustly and unlawfully convicted. I didn't give Miss Jursmar any instructions concerning the trials. I thought perhaps she herself would feel it necessary to use them to petition for their liberation. No one is forbidden to intercede for his friends. As a Christian, I'm free to do this. There are many instances in the Bible where believers exposed illegalities, intervened on behalf of their friends and petitioned the authorities. Esther went to the king to intercede for her people. Depending on the circumstances, the Apostles endured beatings and persecutions silently in some cases, in others appealed to the law. To petition for prisoners unjustly convicted is not against Soviet law, nor is it against my own convictions.

I attended trials in Moscow and Ryazan. At the one in Ryazan four believers were being tried. On of the defendants was old (aged 71), ill, but an incredibly nice person. He talked to the procurator and the judge in an old-fashioned, good-natured way, in such a homely tone of voice. It was very moving and made the illegality of the whole trial the more repellant. Sitting there in the court-room, I wanted the whole world to see what was going on there. Then perhaps those who were infringing the law would be ashamed of what they were doing and stop. Their actions were so repellent. An old man, quite innocent . . .

[*At this point the Procurator interrupts Aida, accusing her once again of pronouncing false and slanderous statements against the USSR. Aida strongly denies that anything she has said is either false or slanderous: she claims, therefore, that she is not guilty.*

On Monday 15 *July the third and last day of her trial takes place. Here is what Aida said in her final speech:*—]

First of all I want to say – I started to talk about this on Friday, but for some reason I was not allowed to finish – I applied in writing to the City Court asking for permission to have a Bible with me. Then lawyer Denisov came to me and said I would be given a Bible after the trial. He said definitely that I would be given one, not that this question would be settled. Now I ask that this promise be fulfilled.

Citizen judges! Everyone knows what a joy it is to have a loving mother. People have different conceptions of happiness and joy in life. For some happiness is a life free of cares, for others their idea of joy is to go to the theatre, etc. But none of this can be compared to the happiness of having a loving mother. This is a special, higher conception of happiness, as everybody knows. I'm telling you this so that you realize that I have the same kind of happiness in being able to call God my Heavenly Father – and suddenly I have come to understand the meaning of this relationship more clearly than ever before. Heavenly Father – this means that I can turn to Him with my needs, tell Him everything, ask Him about everything and entrust my life to Him. The fact that I can call God my Father is very precious to me. . . . We are God's slaves because we desire to serve God humbly and put ourselves at His disposal. Christ said, "Henceforth I call you not servants; for the servant knoweth not what his Lord doeth: but I have opened up the way for you. You are friends!" Yes, we are slaves and friends and children. Atheism, now there's a really evil slavery. Take this trial. What have I seen in this trial? Once again I have seen that people are increasingly losing an understanding of what is just and reasonable. I've already quoted Lenin's words in my defence speech: "Of the European countries, only in Russia and Turkey were shameful laws against religious people still in force. These laws either directly prohibited the open profession of faith or forbade its propagation. These laws are the most unjust, shameful and oppressive." At one time people realized that it is unjust to forbid the propagation of a faith, now they don't understand this. Now they say, "Believe yourself and pray, but don't dare talk about God to anyone." To silence one's ideological opponent by force is no ideological victory. This has always been called barbarism.

Procurator: A propos of what is she introducing this quotation from Lenin? Lenin was talking about Tsarist times.

(The judge banged the table with the palm of the hand, calling the Procurator to order.)

Aida: I don't know whether any parents ever before used to be forbidden to bring up their children according to their convictions, or if so, when. Now they are even encroaching on this sacred right of parents. This trial is horrifying but not because you're going to pass sentence on me and take me off to prison. It's horrifying because many of those sitting in the court-room will not realize that it is unjust. I have been telling you why I sent the magazines *Herald of Salvation* and *Fraternal Leaflet* abroad. What is happening in the life of our church is a miracle. In the twentieth century, when atheists are shouting about the extinguishing of faith, a fire like this suddenly flares up. And I wanted everybody to know about this miracle of awakening.

The Church upholds truth and fights for the truth.

Judge: You are not to talk about the church; talk about yourself.

Aida: I'll talk about myself in a minute. The Church's struggle is not to be understood as some political battle. The Church's struggle is to stand in the way of truth and follow the Lord straightforwardly, regardless of everything else. When the Church is fighting I can't remain uninvolved. One can be a militant atheist or a non-militant atheist, one can be simply a non-believer, indifferent towards both faith and atheism, but for the Christian there is only one course. The Christian can't be anything but militant. Once you know the truth, this means following it, upholding it and if necessary suffering for it. I can't be different. I can't act any differently.

There has been talk here about the fact that we communicate with people abroad. The Council of Prisoners' Relatives sent a letter to U Thant at the United Nations Organization. These were mothers and wives of prisoners, writing about their children and husbands, unjustly convicted. One can understand them; I don't know how anyone could decide to condemn them. I know one mother – her son's in prison – and when she spoke about him I saw tears in her eyes, such restrained tears, they were in the depths of her eyes. A week before her arrest I met another mother – a believer called Sloboda. You know, they wrote about her in the letter to U Thant; two of her daughters were taken away from her. The children had already been in a children's home for a year, when they suddenly ran away quite unexpectedly. They had to take a train or a bus, I don't remember which, and then they ran for two kilometres. They ran home in such heavy frost that their mother was frightened. "Weren't you really frozen?" she asked. But the children replied, "We kept on running and running, we stopped, rubbed our knees and ran on again." The mother asked the younger girl, "Didn't you cry a bit from the cold?" – "What are you thinking about, mummy?" said the litle girl, amazed. "How could we cry at such a happy time? After all, we were running home!" The children lived at home for a month and didn't want to go to bed without their mother, so all that time they slept in the same bed as their mother. But then they were taken away again to the children's home.

I'm not in any way an important figure, and I'm not a heroine. I love freedom and would very much like to be free now with my family and friends. But I can't buy freedom at any price; I don't want to act against my conscience. I love freedom, but what good is freedom to me if I can't call God my Father? In prison one particular verse became especially dear to me and precious:

"Oh no, no one in the whole universe can rob the faithful of freedom,
Though flesh fear the prisoner's chain and prison fill it with dismay,
For the God of love gave freedom to Thought enslaved by darkness,
And hitherto the world has not forged chains for her, the liberated one."

The knowledge that my soul and thoughts are free encourages and strengthens me. That is all I wanted to say to you.'

VII

AN INTERVIEW WITH AIDA

(Anonymous, written by a Western friend in 1971)

PEOPLE IN different parts of the world have shown concern for what has happened to the young Christian girl in the USSR, Aida Mikhailovna Skripnikova. She has been in prison twice for confessing the name of Jesus. The first time she was sentenced to one year's imprisonment from 1965-1966. The second term of punishment was three years, 1968-1971.

Now Aida is free again. The heavy gates of the labour camp opened for her on 12 April 1971. The long days have passed, for the time being.

How is Aida? What does she look like? She is young, about 30 years old. Aida is a brown-eyed Russian girl of slender build. Her eyes express joy and peacefulness. Her prison-mates trusted and loved her. Aida does not talk about the difficulties and tribulation she experienced, but about God's wonderful protection, peace and joy.

"I was released from the labour camp on 12 April. We were not set free directly from the camp, but were transferred at first to another place. There we lived for two weeks. There they told me that I was a person who had learned nothing from her punishment. Therefore they didn't give me a passport, as they did to the other prisoners. I received only a paper, which indicated that I had been released from prison after serving my complete sentence. The place where I have to live is quite a large town, east of Moscow. Only when I go there will I get my passport. I'm not allowed to be outside after 9 o'clock in the evening. Twice a week I have to report to the local police to show I'm in town. I can't travel outside the town without permission from the police. This rule is in force for six months. If I don't mend my ways after that time, the same rules will remain in force for another six months. Then, after that I don't know what will happen. If I don't obey the rules imposed on me, they can arrest me again at any time. Usually such hard rules are imposed only on criminals, murderers and hooligans. It appears that I'm counted among such people."

When she left the camp, Aida was told that she had not been reformed, nor had she altered her views. "I asked them what kind of improvement they wished to see in me. The man then read the thoughts which I had written down in a notebook confiscated by them. He asked me: "Don't you realize that those who bring Bibles to the Soviet Union are only trying to harm us?" I told him that if we had Bibles in Russia and there were no Bibles in Sweden, I'd be prepared to be the first one to take Bibles there."

When asking Aida what she felt was the most difficult aspect of life in prison, she hesitated for a little while. It was a hard question to answer, as could be seen from her face. Finally she answered with a smile.

"Firstly, it was very difficult to be separated from one's friends. Secondly, it was hard being cut off from the world; you couldn't go anywhere. However, the hardest thing was to live without the Gospel. After having spent some time in prison, I asked for a Bible, but they woudn't give me one. A sister brought me the Gospel of St. Mark. The guards, when they learned that I had a Gospel, were frightened. A search of the camp was organized. Twice they arranged a thorough search for the Gospel and the second time they found it. For that I got ten days and nights in solitary confinement, in the cold detention cell of the prison.

"A couple of weeks after this incident I succeeded in getting the whole New Testament into my prison. I managed to keep the book almost till the day of my release. Many times the guards organized searches. The Lord helped me every time: I was able to discover in advance when there was to be a search and hide this precious book. Many of my prisonmates helped to hide it, although they were not Christians. Just before my release they took away from me all the notes I'd written during my time there. Nothing that I'd written during those three years was left.

"Although prison conditions were very hard", said Aida, "hope remained with me. I experienced no sorrow, my spirit was not depressed by fear. I was able to live through those three years with the words from St. Mathew, chapter 11, verse 30 before my eyes: 'For my yoke is easy and my burden is light'. Though these words from the Bible were very familiar to me before my arrest, only now do I understand how true and correct they are. Christ's burden is indeed light to bear. I experienced this in a deep way in prison many times. During my time there I had a wonderful friend, the risen Lord Jesus Christ. I experienced in prison the same as did a Christian sister, who wrote from her cell that Christ gives His grace and presence to those in prison, so that one is able to endure what lies ahead. We're never alone or rejected, not even in prison."

Aida is only one of those who have suffered for Christ's sake. She is known all over the world. When Aida was told that a postcard had been printed with her picture and distributed in different parts of the world in thousands of copies, she was confused. She said she was happy that people had remembered her. "However, this is how I understand why people have remembered me: they remember me as a representative of all suffering Christians, and when remembering me they are remembering all the Lord's witnesses, who suffer in different parts of the world for the sake of their Master.

"In prison I received many greeting cards and parcels. Once I was told that I'd received ten parcels from Norway, but they refused to give them to me, because I hadn't altered my convictions. I don't know who sent these parcels, but I would like to express my gratitude to everyone who prayed both for me and my brothers and sisters who share the same fate as I. Once, when I was shown a package and told that it contained chocolate and other good things, I found that I didn't need the contents. I gained much greater blessing from the fact that my friends cared for me.

"All this concern for me I looked upon as meant for all of us and not just for me. The most marvellous thing is that nothing can separate believers from each other. All those who belong to the Lord are one body, wherever they be and in whatever conditions. Some people think that Christians in closed countries are cut off from contact with the rest of the Lord's family. Therefore it is a great joy for us to experience concrete, visible spiritual communion with Christians living in different parts of the world. From this we receive hope in prison. I would like to send an expression of love from us all to those who have cared for us and prayed for us.

"The task of prayer doesn't end when a person is released from prison. We continually need prayer. My wish is that all Christians should unite to pray for each other. We ought to pray that our faith will remain unbroken, whatever the external conditions of our lives."

Aida's own person assures us of the trustworthiness of her words. She had lost her life and found it, found her life in Christ, who is Almighty and who is already victorious now. The Lord has given no man power over another person's soul. They can destroy the body, but that is nothing to be afraid of. Fear Him who has power to decide the eternal fate of man. Before Him every knee shall bow; even they who have denied Him will kneel.

VIII

EPILOGUE: MARTYRS OF RELIGIOUS PROTEST

This article appeared in Sunday Telegraph *of 28 May* 1972. *It was written by the "Close-up Team" –Michael Bourdeaux, Stephen Constant, Elga Eliaser, David Floyd, John Miller and Ronald Payne. It is reproduced here because it shows, firstly, that many others are now prepared to stand on ground which was first liberated by Aida Skripnikov in the early* 1960'*s; secondly, it illustrates the increasing diversity of Christian people now struggling to achieve religious freedom in the Soviet Union.*

The publication of this article in a major newspaper – the first time in history that there has been such a long report on Christianity in the USSR – itself shows that at last the Western world is begining to realize just how important a role religion continues to play in Russia.

So it was with Aida. So it is with thousands – more probably millions – of people of all denominations in the USSR, for whom the joy of the Risen Christ, their personal knowledge of their Saviour, is the great reality of their lives.

Tertullian, looking back on three centuries of tribulation under the Romans, shortly before Constantine accepted the new faith as the religion of the empire, said: "The more you persecute us, the more we grow. The blood of the martyrs is the seed of the church." Those words are still true in the 1970'*s. While the full story of Russia's modern martyrs remains to be written, this account of some events in Aida Skripnikova's early years shows she will deserve a chapter in it.*

WORKING IN a Siberian labour camp this Sunday morning are two middle-aged Baptists, a man and a woman. They were sent there as a punishment for the grave offence of handing out Bibles and teaching the Lord's Prayer to Russian children.

Their action and the punishment it brought stand token for

an important element in the protest movement in Russia today and the way the State reacts to it. Religious dissidence has its own martyrs and its own underground propagation of the faith through *samizdat* or self-publication.

Every Soviet believer has the constitutional right to organize and take part in religious worship. For good measure the Government has signed the Universal Declaration of Human Rights adopted by the General Assembly of the United Nations in 1948, article 18 of which runs: "Everyone has the right to freedom of thought, conscience and religion; this right includes freedom . . . to manifest his religion or belief in teaching, practice, worship and observance."

Despite this, hundreds of citizens have been arrested for preaching the Gospel. Particularly during the past 12 years a bitter and little-publicized anti-religious campaign has been conducted by the State. Its special target has been the Baptist Church, with perhaps three million members, but it also oppresses the Russian Orthodox Church, the Roman Catholics, and sects such as Jehovah's Witnesses. In spite of the persecutions there are still three and a half million Catholics, and the Orthodox Church claims to have as many as 30 million adherents.

The churches in Russia are tolerated only within strict limits. The law bans religious organizations from taking part in social and cultural activities, they may not do charitable work, and they are forbidden to organize biblical, literary or social groups. They cannot set up playgrounds for children, and they may not even organize church outings.

On the one hand the State "guarantees" freedom of worship; it also underwrites freedom of anti-religious propaganda. And under this heading good party members are encouraged to knock religion as hard as they can.

The two Baptists now serving sentence in Siberia were only recently put on trial in the small Western Ukrainian town of Nikolaev. The trial was held in secret, but another Baptist illegally took notes of what was said in court and the transcript was smuggled out of the Soviet Union. This document is the source for the story which follows.

Georgi Zheltonozhko and Nadya Troshchenko were two factory workers, converted to the Baptist faith, whose fervour led them to break with the "official" and recognized Baptist

Church and join the *Initsiativniki*, an action group of reformist evangelical Baptists. The original Baptist Church was firmly established in pre-revolutionary Russia by German and British influences. Its simple Bible Christianity appeals strongly to workers and to people in labour camps, and its reformist wing in particular has long been in trouble with authority. In the past decade no fewer than 600 Baptists have been imprisoned and nearly 200 are still inside.

The trial of Georgi Zheltonozhko and Nadya Troshchenko lasted three days. Georgi was charged with receiving and distributing "Bibles, New Testaments and other spiritual literature, thereby trampling on Soviet laws," and with holding prayer meetings at his home.

It is highly likely that the literature bore the imprint "Christian publishing house," an organization which on its clandestine press has been producing Bibles, hymn books and magazines. This has been one of the most daring and effective way of protest by the break-away Baptists. The movement's illegal journal *Fraternal Leaflet* made its first appearance in 1965 and was hand-written and mimeographed. But since last year it has been offset printed, and the K.G.B. have so far failed to shut down the illegal printing works.

To the annoyance of the Government some 40,000 New Testaments and hymn books have been run off and circulated to Baptists throughout the Soviet Union. It is the movement's way of replying to the Government's refusal to print religious works for them, or give them permission to do it themselves.

It was for receiving this "illegal" literature from Georgi that Nadya Troshchenko found herself in court. It was further alleged that she had read New Testament stories and poems to children, and that she had made them kneel in prayer.

At the beginning of the trial the judge asked Georgi: "Did you import and distribute literature?"

"Yes, and I gave it to everybody," replied Georgi, who had already refused to accept help from defence counsel on the grounds that "Truth does not need any defence."

Judge: "Where is it printed?"

Georgi: "Praise God, I don't know."

"Why did you do this?"

"According to Lenin's decree on religion, citizens are permitted not only to believe, but also to confess their faith and propagate it. Lenin granted freedom, he didn't limit it; the same is true of the United Nations convention on human rights."

He complained to the judge about the coarse behaviour of Soviet officials who broke up a prayer meeting he had organized. Some were drunk, and they insulted the believers and called them rabble.

"You tell us to preach only in a house of prayer. The Lord says: 'Go into all the world and preach the Gospel'."

Judge: "The Gospels were written a long time ago, they can change like our laws according to circumstances. The Bible was written for those times; today the author would have written something different."

At this point the prosecutor intervened. "If I have read my Romans right I find at 13.2 it says 'Obey the authorities'."

Georgi: "The answer to that is Ephesians 6.12 – 'We are not contending against flesh and blood but against the principalities, against the powers, against the world rulers of this present darkness.' We are fulfilling the law of Christ, the Gospel, which says 'Who should we obey, man or God?'; the lesser yields to the greater. I submit to God; to whom do you submit?"

Nadya Troshchenko was formally charged at this point with gathering children together, reading the New Testament and poems to them, and teaching them prayers. The judge asked, "Do you plead guilty?"

Nadya: "No! Christ said 'Suffer the little children to come unto me'."

Judge: "Children can choose for themselves after the age of 18, but you are brainwashing schoolchildren of eleven or twelve years old."

Nadya: "But before they have to choose their own path they should be taught both sides. No parents can abandon their children to ruin and death."

Judge: "Did you read the New Testament to children and do you intend to continue to do so?"

Nadya: "Yes, in the presence of their parents. As for the future, I hope I needn't read the New Testament to them any more. I hope they will read it to me."

A twelve-year-old boy called as a witness "confessed" to kneeling with Nadya and to saying the Lord's Prayer. He was asked to repeat the words of the prayer before the court, which he did. He then burst into tears and was sent outside.

Finally Georgi was given an opportunity to speak in his own defence. "You are trying me for my faith and not for breaking the law," he said. "Our faith cannot be contained only in a church building. Faith without works is dead, as a body is dead without the spirit."

He accused the authorities of not allowing children to be brought up in a Christian spirit. "You start educating children into Communist movements. We have to train our children too, because when they grow up it may be too late to tell them about God. I lost twenty-seven years before being converted, and I don't want to see them do the same."

Nadya also defended herself. "In the laws on religion," she said, "it is forbidden to speak the word of God except in church and it is forbidden to teach children. That means that faith itself is prohibited. A Communist needs the party rule book and a Christian needs the New Testament and spiritual literature. The Bible is tolerated in our country, yet you cannot buy one in a shop."

In conclusion she said: "Our Lord teaches us to love everyone, not to hate. Whatever sentence you give us I will pray that the Lord may open your eyes."

Georgi Zheltonozhko was sent to a labour camp for three years. Nadya Troshchenko got eighteen months for teaching the Bible to children.

"What about our children – should we inspire in them a love of the Church or not? Yes . . ." Alexander Solzhenitsyn, winner of the 1970 Nobel Prize for Literature, made this defiant assertion in his Lenten letter to Patriarch Pimen, head of the Russian Orthodox Church, which was published in *The Sunday Telegraph* on 9 April 1972.

Many people seem surprised to hear such an affirmation of the Christian faith from one of the Soviet Union's outstanding personalities fifty-four years after the State adopted a policy of atheism. But Solzhenitsyn had made his Christian sympathies known years ago, and thousands of other Russians have been writing and signing such letters for more than a decade.

Solzhenitsyn made two points which reinforce the protests of many other Russian Christians, Orthodox, Roman Catholic and Protestant. First, many Christians are denied any possibility of worshipping legally, because there are vast areas where the Soviet authorities refuse to licence churches. Second, the present leadership of the Churches is not strong enough in resisting the State's control of church life.

Both these points have been consistently made by Russian Christians for more than a decade. Years before Soviet Jews began addressing the outside world, Russian Christians were putting their case for religious freedom logically, coolly and with a wealth of documented fact.

The Russian Baptists began to write letters of protest in 1960 when Khruschev inspired the most vigorous anti-religious campaign since the early 1930s. They have indeed been protesting against persecution for their religious beliefs for nearly one hundred years. Their history has made them resilient and has left them with a keen memory of the strength of evangelical Christianity in the world outside.

Their numbers grew in adversity to an estimated three million in the late 1950s, and since then many have been converted. Baptists protested strongly when the Government began closing churches, imprisoning religious leaders and generally putting intolerable pressure upon young people who showed even a passing interest in the Christian faith. These churchmen appealed in turn to the leaders of their own denomination, the State authorities, their co-religionists outside the country and finally to the United Nations and other international bodies. Their case was that they and countless other believers wished to be loyal to their country, but were being forced to act illegally, because the Soviet authorities would not license religious worship for thousands of Christian groups all over the Soviet Union. Where registration was granted this meant submitting to a surveillance which was unacceptable. Countless people could not enjoy even that minimal degree of religious freedom which the Soviet constitution was supposed to guarantee.

The violent reaction of the State against these protests was perhaps predictable. The reaction from the Moscow Baptist Church leadership and the lack of it from the Church in general was more surprising.

The Baptist leadership in Russia had already compromized itself in the eyes of many believers by accepting a "letter of instruction" from the State which went beyond the law in the restrictions on evangelism and work with young people.

Surprisingly the All-Union Council of Evangelical Christians and Baptists ruled that "an elder presbyter must be clearly aware of and remember the main objective of divine service nowadays is not to attract new members" (that is to say they should refrain from finding new members). It also decreed that an elder presbyter had the duty of suppressing "unhealthy missionary phenomena" – meaning that such people should not proselytize.

These and other compromising edicts split the Protestant movement in Russia. (Solzhenitsyn himself complained about similar compromise in the Orthodox Church.) A considerable number of rank-and-file Baptists broke with their leaders. In the end the Church leadership had to rescind the offending "letter of instruction," but the damage had been done.

The driving force of the reform Baptists in the past few years has been the Council of Baptist Prisoners' Relatives. Despite the arest of successive groups of leading members, the Council collected precise information about Baptists in prison and sent a series of letters to the United Nations, but without any result.

John Miller, then in Moscow, talked to a breakaway Baptist, Mrs. Yakimenkova at House 84, Desna Village, in the Leninsky District of the Moscow Region, who was one of five women to write to U Thant, UN Secretary General, after their menfolk had been arrested. On a bitterly cold day he found her in a simple wooden house without water or electricity. In the living room, furnished with only a table, two chairs and a cupboard, was Mrs. Yakimenkova with her mother and two small children.

For holding illegal prayer meetings there her husband was serving a two-year prison-camp sentence. Once convinced that her visitor was not a KGB agent, Mrs. Yakimenkova began to weep and spoke freely about the unhappy life of a Soviet Protestant. "Tell the United Nations that we hear nothing from them," she said. "Our prayer meetings are broken up by the police. They send our men to the camps. We, the wives, our aged parents and our children are left to die from starvation."

The Baptists are encouraged by the thought that more people outside are at last prepared to sponsor their cause. A concerted movement of Western public opinion like that which has sustained the Jews could help them enormously, and in this cause a day of prayer for Eastern Europe has been organized for 4 June. It is sponsored by the British-based Centre for the Study of Religion and Communism.

A parallel movement of protest within the Russian Orthodox Church was begun by two priests, Father Nikolai Eshliman and Father Gleb Yakunin, with the support of Archbishop Yermogen. The priests wrote an open letter to the Government requesting that religious freedom tolerated under the law should be allowed in fact. Another letter complained that the Church leadership had failed to take a sufficiently strong stand against the illegal inroads of atheism. For this they were dismissed. Archbishop Yermogen made a similar approach to the Patriarch, and is now in enforced retirement.

Here, perhaps, is the greatest tragedy of Christian life in Russia today – the State has such a hold over the Church that it bars the most worthy from office. This is not to say that all bishops and official Baptist leaders are traitors to the Gospel. Many of them struggle to keep their church afloat and sustain a ministry of high quality, as Archbishop Yermogen did until 1965. Nevertheless, the pressures of atheism are tremendous, and they lead some individuals and groups into sorry postures.

Last year the *Sobor* (General Council) of the Russian Orthodox Church met for the first time since 1945. Metropolitan Pimen became Patriarch (there was no other candidate) and the Church signally failed to raise any of the most crucial problems which confront it – lack of sufficient theological education, religious books, and parish churches in thousands of towns and villages, and the inability of the priest to control matters in his own parish because of the current regulations putting all administrative matter in the hands of a council of laity (whose membership is itself controlled by the atheist authorities, according to Soviet law). The only mention of such problems was in a gathering exclusively for bishops the day before the *Sobor* officially convened. This meeting was uncanonical, but at least it had the merit of containing some freedom of speech, which was totally absent from the monumental boredom of the set speeches.

Before the Revolution Russia had some 80,000 Orthodox churches, chapels and monasteries. Perhaps only about 8,000 still function today. Church leaders are reluctant to give figures. All they will say is that there are eight Metropolitans, thirty Archbishops, thirty-five Bishops, and two ecclesiastical academies and three seminaries.

The Soviet Government's attitude to religion is to say there is nothing to worry about because the congregations consist largely of elderly people. But evidence reaching the West suggests that for the first time in one hundred years younger people and especially intellectuals are beginning to return to the fold.

One remarkable example is provided by the case history of Sergei Kourdakov, a twenty-two-year-old from the Kamchatka area of the Soviet Far East who is now in Canada. As a zealous Komsomol (Young Communist) leader he was a part-time KGB informer, and he specialized in harrying the Baptists in his district.

For Kourdakov the moment of revelation came one night last year when he and his friends broke into a clandestine prayer meetings.

"There was one old lady there who kept on praying as we set about them. I was so angry that I was about to do her in. I raised my hand. Then I realized that she was not praying for herself – she was praying that God might forgive me. Suddenly I felt somebody holding my fist in check. There was nobody, but I knew there must be something special there."

Kourdakov became a Christian and went to sea as a radio operator. He jumped ship and chose freedom in Canada.

Another Soviet weapon against the spread of religion is confinement in an asylum for the insane. A document in *samizdat* about this, called "Notes from the Red House," recently reached the West. Its author is Gennady Shimanov, who was incarcerated in the notorious Kashchenko mental hospital in Moscow as a "semi-violent" patient.

One of his doctor-interrogators said to him: "If you had grown up in a religious family or had lived somewhere in the West, well, then we could have looked at your religiousness in another way. But you were educated in a Soviet school and were brought up in a family of non-believers. You are an educated person, I'm ready to admit that you know more about philosophy and religion than I do. And suddenly – snap – you're religious!

"Your symptoms are a one-sided fascination with religion. You've cut yourself off from life. After all, how do healthy believers behave? An old dear pops into church, crosses herself, goes away and gets on with other things. Already she has forgotten about God. There are still such people, but they are getting fewer. With you it is quite different. We are worried about you."

Religion, it seems, is aceptable to the regime so long as it can be seen to by dying out.

Throughout his time in the mental hospital Shimanov, a distinguished army officer cashiered for his Christian belief, showed himself a tough nut to crack. He devoted himself to proving that it is possible to be "normal" and at the same time a devout Christian. It took a hunger strike to free him. As soon as he was outside again he bravely used his notes of the interrogation to write and publish a full account of his time in the mental hospital.

The Roman Catholics, like the Jews, were victims of oppression in Russia long before the Communists took over. Imperial Russia feared the Roman Church as a powerful rival to Orthodoxy and an undesirable foreign influence. The Soviets saw the Vatican as a threat to their dream of world Communism. They feared its political authority, spiritual discipline and implacable opposition to the godless State.

Catholicism might have been stamped out as a result of ruthless persecution between the two World Wars had not the Red Army seized Lithuania, Latvia and Eastern Poland, all areas with large Catholic populations.

Before 1940 Lithuania had three million people, of whom 80 per cent were Catholics. Almost half the churches have since been closed. The number of priests fell from 1,500 in 1940 to about 800 at the end of the 1960s. There are only four active bishops instead of fourteen, and two others are under permanent house arrest.

An appeal in March to Mr. Brezhnev, the party leader, was signed by 17,000 Lithuanian Catholics and sent directly to Dr. Waldheim, the new United Nations Secretary General, as previous appeals had never reached the Kremlin leaders. It was explained that there would have been many more signatures but police had detained collectors and seized lists. The appeal said: "We expect such effort from the Government as will help us Catholics to regard ourselves as citizens of the Soviet Union with equal rights."

This appeal fell on deaf ears. Ten days ago the upsurge of religious feeling in that part of the Soviet Empire, coupled with renascent nationalist aspirations, led to bloodshed in the streets.

Young Lithunanians clashed with Russian troops in the streets of Kaunas, the second largest city in the republic, after a twenty-year-old Roman Catholic factory worker named Roman Kalanta had burned himself to death in a public park. His gesture had both religious and political motives.

What brought the crowds out to shout "Freedom for Lithuania" was frustration and resentment kindled by such incidents as the arrest last summer of a Roman Catholic priest, Father Zdebskis. Six KGB men broke in and took him as he was preparing children for their first Communion.

He spent more than two months in prison awaiting trial, and was beaten.

Although the authorities tried to keep the date of the hearing secret, 600 people gathered outside the district court on the day. Reports smuggled out described the scene:

"Many girls brought flowers. But the militia moved in to break up the crowd. One woman had a rib broken, another fell unconscious from a blow on the head. Women and girls were beaten and dragged to police cars."

Father Zdebskis was sentenced to a year in an internment camp.

Another group of Eastern-rite Catholics probably numbering about four million, who came under Soviet rule with the annexation of the Western Ukraine in 1939, has been equally repressed. They have never fitted either into the Orthodox or the Catholic framework, but as they owe an allegiance to Rome they are highly suspect to the Kremlin. Their churches and schools have either passed into Orthodox hands or been closed, but the Church continues to flourish underground.

Other religious minorities such as the Seventh-Day Adventists, the Pentecostals and the Jehovah's Witnesses have also suffered badly during the recurring anti-religious campaigns, particularly during the "black years" of the Krushchev era.

These sects are treated as nothing more or less than fanatical underground political movements. But they survive.

One of the most colourful characters in the Christian wing of the protest movement in Russia is Anatoli Levitin, a teacher and literary scholar.

Since 1959 Levitin has been a frequent and bold contributor to *samizdat* on religious themes, and particularly against violations of religious freedom. He has spoken out against constant interference by the authorities in the life of the Church and against the unchecked power of elders appointed by the State. His special target has been the Orthodox Church hierarchy itself for quietly acquiescing to State edicts.

Levitin was quick to see that freedom was indivisible and that there could be no religious freedom if basic human rights were curtailed. Throughout the late 1960s he organized protests on behalf of young Russians arrested for political offences and saw to it that they were aired in *samizdat*. It was, of course, only a question of time before Levitin's protests were stifled. Last year he began a three-year sentence in a labour camp for "anti-Soviet activities".

✠ ✠ ✠

To witness an Easter liturgy in the Russian Orthodox Church is to experience a spiritual reality which renders the question "Can religion survive in Russia?" purely academic.

The procession of clergy and deacons walks around the church, looking for the body of Christ. Not finding him, they fling open the door of the darkened church and ask where he is. "He is not here. He is risen – *Khristos voskres*!" comes back the answer.

A few voices inside the church take up the call – *Khristos voskres* – at first murmuring as though in disbelief. Then more and more voices join in, until it becomes a triumphant shout. The choirs reaffirm the news in jubilation.

As the volume swells, so the light in the church becomes brighter. First, only a single point of light, then two – then more and more, as the faithful light their candles and pass the flame from one to another.

Each one is a pool of light which frames the face. On that face is the affirmation of faith achieved through suffering. For them resurrection is not something to be argued about, it is a reality here and now, the most positive experience of their lives.

POSTSCRIPT

In September 1972 news was received about Aida Skripnikova: she was working at a train depot in Leningrad, cleaning railway carriages and trucks, and had received a cut in her wages. It was claimed that she was in great danger, since the authorities were preparing yet another case against her.

In November 1972 Aida's contemporary, Yuri Galanskov, died in prison at the age of 33. This outstanding Christian gave his life for his ideals of freedom.

FOR FURTHER INFORMATION

Readers are referred to the paperback, *Faith on Trial in Russia*, by Michael Bourdeaux (Hodder and Stoughton), (45p, post paid). This gives fuller information about the reform Baptist movement, concentrating on the leaders, Georgi Vins and Gennadi Kryuchkov.

Religious Minorities in the Soviet Union 1960-70 (40p., post paid) gives more general information about Soviet policy towards religion.

Both these are available from the Centre for the Study of Religion and Communism (CSRC) which has compiled the present book. This is a new organization, registered under the Department of Education and Science as a charity, which seeks to circulate objective and factual information about religion in the Communist countries to individuals, universities and churches. It publishes a journal, *Religion in Communist Societies* (annual subscription £2).

All enquiries and book orders to:

CSRC,
34 Lubbock Road,
Chislehurst,
Kent BR7 5JJ.